MAKING MUSIC FUN:

a complete collection
of games, puzzles
and activities for
the elementary classroom

Also by the Authors:

Elementary Teacher's Music Almanack: Timely Lesson Plans for Every Day of the School Year

MAKING MUSIC FUN:

a complete collection
of games, puzzles
and activities for
the elementary classroom

Marvin S. Adler
and
Jesse C. McCarroll

PARKER PUBLISHING COMPANY, INC.
WEST NYACK, NEW YORK

© 1981

PARKER PUBLISHING COMPANY, INC.

West Nyack, New York

Library of Congress Cataloging in Publication Data

Adler, Marvin Stanley.
  Making music fun.

  Includes index.
  1. School music—Instruction and study.
I. McCarroll, Jesse C.
MT10.A195   372.8'7044   81-94 74
                                AACR2

ISBN 0-13-547455-8

Printed in the United States of America

To Trevor, Polly, Maxine,
Mark and June,
and the Lincoln Center Institute

Let us all attend to
Active encounters
with the entire
artistic-aesthetic
domain.

Acknowledgments

The authors are particularly indebted to Herbert Bender for creating the book jacket design and to Jorge Sicre, of the Cleveland Orchestra, for the illustrations found in the book.

We would like to extend our appreciation to the many friends and persons in the music profession who are a continuous source of inspiration and encouragement: Paul Ash, President of Music Belongs; Alfred Balkin, Western Michigan University; Emmanuel Gioldasis, Robert H. Lee, Andrew P. Velez, and Camille C. Taylor of New York City; Michael V. W. Gordon, Indiana University; Joseph Sugar, President of the New York State School Music Association; Robert F. Holden, New York City Technical College (CUNY). Leonard Robertson and students of classes 8M-4 and 8P-4 of the Jackie Robinson Intermediate School, Brooklyn, New York, were instrumental in the creation, testing, and evaluation of teaching ideas used in this book.

Finally, very special thanks to Ms. Muriel Adler and Mark Adler for the many hours they spent helping to research material for this book. Without their dedication, devotion, and encouragement, this book would have taken longer to complete.

M. S. A.
J. C. M.

How to Make Music Fun— What This Book Will Do for You

One need only watch a group of youngsters at a party or informal gathering, or clustering around a juke box, to know that young people don't need *US* to have *fun with music*! Then why the "turn-off" in many schools? What is it that we do to hamper their enjoyment? Perhaps an artificial boundary is established. This book is needed because all too often, pupils know that music is fun *outside* of school but not *in* school.

This book will help you make all kinds of music fun in school. Learning about symphonies, chamber and program music *can* be fun! All that is needed is for the music to be approached with humor (often the same humor with which the work was created). Similarly, limericks, jokes, cartoons, anecdotes, skits, pantomime, "daffynitions," satire, charade, and funny lyrics, are all natural paths to a light-hearted presentation of even the most profound, serious works. One of the main reasons for this book is to demonstrate that you can start out having fun with music—even making fun of it at times—and yet wind up with a truly serious approach to the subject. Even great composers—Beethoven and Schubert included—enjoyed poking fun at themselves.

Through the world of humor, you can often help your students become musically responsive to sounds around them, and the many other aspects of music such as textures, tempos, meters, modes, dynamics and harmony. By using this book, your students will become enthusiastic about school music education because you will use novelty and excitement to capture their attention and stimulate their interest.

Another value of this book is to provide you with a great variety of practical ideas and activities, complete with instructions on how to make music fun. (There are both group and individualized adventures into the world of music; activities that are highly structured as well as those that are flexible and "open.") And we say complete because, along with additions to many well-known types of games and puzzles, we have added limericks, gags, pantomimes, cartoons, and many other activities that go along with having funny experiences—and fun! Hundreds of ideas are provided for ways in which you and your class can further expand upon these activities. You can learn how to use poetry, mathematics, science, history and geography. Music can be interwoven with other disciplines for optimal fun.

Activities were collected from all types of students, all types of teachers, supervisors and clinicians, and from all over the country. Dozens of classroom-tested approaches have emerged from an evaluation process that included selecting out those lessons which children themselves have found to be boring.

Teachers related that they used music at focal points during the year such as Halloween, Thanksgiving, Christmas, or Easter. The purpose of this book is to enable you to use music more often—to widen the base; to broaden the number of times you think of music as part of the three R's (Reading, 'Riting, and Rhythm).

We have found that every aspect of musical activity can be made enjoyable—singing, dancing, playing instruments, learning to read notes, rhythmic and melodic dictation. Games, puzzles, jokes and other social activities can turn many dry facts into fun. And games are not the only answer, for we have found that students love to draw, love to make things, and love to talk to each other. Why not harness these natural desires? Why not stop fighting them? Why disparage television? Why not utilize a medium that 100 million or more children watch? Programs and commercials are both effective communicators—and more than half of all programs watched are seen for relaxation and FUN.

Here is just a sampling of the many exciting new approaches to be found in this book:

- Activities that enable your students to have fun with conducting and other rhythmic movement.
- Methods of approaching creativity so that it is fun as well as hard work.
- Motivation techniques that make your students eager to learn about instruments.
- Humorous stories to pique curiosity about musicians and music literature.
- Energizers that send your students scurrying about to restructure a room, build scenery, or make posters and display cabinets.
- Games and enrichment ideas for joining together the arts with math, science, and social studies.
- Utilization of most of the things that children normally consider fun.
- Presentation of thoroughly researched ideas from both ends of the spectrum: fresh and dynamic ones from teachers and the students themselves; time-honored ideas from out-of-print books that should not be lost.

• A special section of one-liners, puzzles, and teasers about various aspects of music, in addition to full, detailed activities

Here is what this book can do for you. Every page is packed with ideas that take away the drudgery from teaching music. For the lower grades there is the humor of limericks and cartoons. For the upper grades there is the more sophisticated humor of funny operas, ballets, symphonies, and stories about composers and compositions. Have FUN!

M. S. A.
J. C. M.

Contents

Chapter 4 - Drama, Music, and Fun   59

Chapter 5 - Fun Dances   77

Chapter 6 - Things Found Funny and Funny Sounds   95

Chapter 7 - Crashing Cymbals   113

Chapter 8 - Name That Tune   127

Chapter 9 - Enjoying Listening for a Change   147

Chapter 10 - More Enjoying Listening for a Change 161

Chapter 11 - Sounds, Spelling and Movement 177

Chapter 12 - Mostly Music and Math 197

Chapter 13 - More Music and... 215

Chapter 14 - A Baker's Dozen of Fun Activities 231

Index 241

September:
Back to School

It's a new year and you have decided to use more music. Children have fun with music anyway; why not include some? It makes sense. But, too many teachers have failed by trying to get into note reading right away—too soon; or long classical works too soon; or difficult songs too soon.

This section begins with the musical experiences that are most natural to children: (1) both the old and new songs learned over the summer in scout groups or at camp or with friends; (2) the new recordings that they have been listening to with their friends while away or just hanging around during the long hot days; and (3) new radio stations that might have cropped up during the vacation or the new television themes they have recently been exposed to in the fall previews. All of these are natural experiences for your pupils and experiences with which they have FUN!

CAMP: FUN AND GESTURE OR SCOUT SONGS

Children come back to school in September filled with fun. Some of this fun is in the form of gesture songs which they learn from camp counselors and also from the Boy Scouts or the Girl Scouts. Why not tap this resource? Why not capitalize on the enthusiasm with which children move and tap, clap and snap? Your students will not only have fun, but they will also be sharing the enjoyable experiences they have had. All you have to do is ask your students if they learned any "fun " songs this past summer. You might have some brave students who will come to the front of the room; others might prefer to remain in their seats—but they *will* sing the songs. Pupils who are more bashful can sometimes be encouraged to sing into a cassette tape recorder (either in school or at home).

Here is a song that we learned from a second grader at the St. Thomas School in West Hempstead, New York (see Figure 1). As with many camp songs before it, it deals with a new folk hero—only this folk hero, so to speak, is a movie villain. And, as with many folk stories, its basis is in literature that is not anonymous. Do any of your students know it? Can they figure out which gestures to use?

JAWS

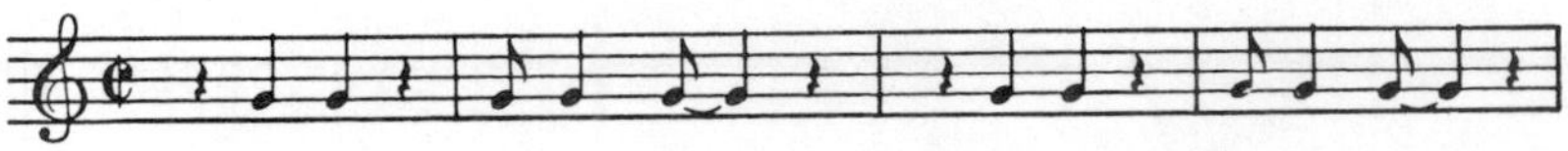

JAWS du du, du du du JAWS du du, du du du

Speak:	Here's a story	du du,	du du du	repeat
	About jaws	"	"	"
	Baby jaws	"	"	"
	Giant jaws	"	"	"
	Lady swimmin'	"	"	"
	Spies the lady	"	"	"
	Shark ahead	"	"	"
	Pass the salt	"	"	"
	And the pepper	"	"	"
	Mmm good	"	"	"
	Swims away	"	"	"
	That's the story	"	"	"
	About jaws	"	"	"

Figure 1

We've omitted some of the lyrics in this song that are risqué. Do your students know them? For obvious reasons, don't let them sing the spicier lyrics in class; just mention that you know of their existence and see if you get any snickers or chuckles. Here's a lesson plan for the same activity.

JAWS

Grades: K - 4

Materials: Words to "Jaws" or any other movement and gesture song learned in camp or from scouting activities.

Concepts:

1. In camp, children learn songs that are considered part of our folklore—even if we know the original authorship.

2. Movement and gesture songs teach perception of *syncopation* (which is displacement of beats and accents in music).

**Activities
&
Directions**

1. Place Figure 1 on the chalkboard. Ask your pupils if any of them know this song. Where did they learn it? In camp? From a counselor? From another child? Do they know a different version of it? Did they see the movie?

2. One of the aspects of the song that is the most fun is putting gestures to it. Which ones can you make up? Which ones do your pupils who already know it use?

3. Syncopation is the displacement or shifting of beats and accents. Without the syncopation in this "Jaws" song, it would not be as much fun to do. It is quite possible that the *du du, du du du* portion of the song has been borrowed from other such songs in the Southern or black American folk tradition. If not, there certainly is the aspect of acculturation that can be discussed with older or intellectually gifted children.

4. There are many, many songs like this one—some very old and many quite new. You might try collecting as many as you and your pupils can. Some can be written down. Others can be collected on cassette tapes. A very interesting aspect of this activity is the fact that current topics are used by children—either made up by them or passed down from child to child. Another interesting discussion you might have is about whether or not the songs were made up or composed by the counselors, or just transmitted by them.

WHAT DID YOU DO ON VACATION?

Grades: 2 - 8

Materials: Recordings involving travel, farm and zoo animals, specific countries, the circus, seasons, rain, rivers, clouds, trees, storms, pets, toys, the ocean, lakes, ships and boats.

Concepts:

1. The summer is a time for relaxation.

2. Music has been written to describe trains, boats, and other methods of travel that we may use during the summer vacation.

3. There are many songs about animals and pets, hiking, nature, the circus, the weather, and other aspects of summertime.

Activities
&
Directions

1. Ask your students what they did over the summer. Try to get a diversity of musical experiences: songs sung, dances learned (popular, folk, and ethnic), records heard, new television and movie music listened to. Try to develop a lively discussion as to what was the most fun. Was it dancing, singing, or just sitting back and listening? Explain that dancing, singing and listening all help one relax. Many music teachers have found that new television and movie music is a good place to start listening activities. Often, it is music with which pupils are already familiar. You then proceed from the known to the unknown.

2. Another enjoyable activity is exposing the children to all sorts of musical materials that can be associated with warm weather and vacation: (a) pet songs such as "How Much Is That Doggie in the Window?"; (b) other recordings about animals such as "Mary Had a Little Lamb," and "Old MacDonald Had a Farm"; (c) the classical *Carnival of the Animals* by Saint-Saëns; circus songs such as "Man on the Flying Trapeze" or the more classical *Circus Band March* by Charles Ives; (d) songs about hiking such as "The Happy Wanderer"; (e) Ferde Grofé's "Cloudburst" from his *Grand Canyon Suite*; (f) Debussy's *Nuages* (Clouds); (g) Gershwin's "Hurricane Scene" from his opera *Porgy and Bess*; Gottschalk's, "Souvenir de Porto Rico"; (h) Debussy's *La Mer* and Delius's *Sea Drift*; "Take Me Out to the Ballgame"; etc. (See *Elementary Teacher's Music Almanack: Timely Lesson Plans for Every Day of the School Year*, Parker Publishing Company, Inc., pp. 23-39 for additional materials and activities regarding coming back to school in September.)

NEW RECORDINGS OVER THE SUMMER

Grades: 3 - 8

Materials: Citizens' Band manuals; recordings that use C.B. expressions; country and western southern rock recordings

Concept:

Children come back to school having had many informal music experiences.

Activities
&
Directions

Summer is a good time for children to catch up on what's new in music. (For you too?) Although there are usually more new dances blossoming in springtime, sometimes the summer also brings on new dance crazes. Children will pick up new steps in camp. City children will pick them up on the street, having more time to just "hang around." What about rural areas that we "city slickers" don't know enough about? Our guess is that some form of "the latest" has gotten "back to the bayou" and "far into the farmyard." Country and Western, and southern rock, became enormously popular in the late 1970's so the dichotomy between city music and country music broke down even further. Long distance short wave radios and citizens' bands "C.B.'s" also helped break down the barriers by spreading speech patterns. You might want to experiment with your class; see how many C.B. expressions they can come up with and list them on the chalkboard. Then ask them to think of songs (pop records) in which they are used. There are many that have worked their way into our general vocabulary like "good buddy!" (So, "what's your handle" and your "20"?)

NEW RADIO STATIONS

Grades: 2 - 8

Materials: A portable radio.

Concept:

The medium is the message.

Activities
&
Directions

Every so often, new radio stations appear. And you are not "hip" if you don't know about them. You should ask your pupils what's new every so often—and really show an interest. It is quite possible that there have been some changes during the long summer period.

Whether in the street, yard, or on the farm, new solid state physics has made hi-fidelity available in portable radio-cassette-record player combinations. A great equalizer! We've started musical discussions by asking students which are the best brands and why.

Have the students share all their reasons for listening to particular radio stations. Many students appear to enjoy their listening session! Yet they have difficulty explaining it in words. Frequent replies are, "they play my kind of music," or "they play our music." Does the "my" mean rock, soul, Hispanic, southern country or what? Do you have other ethnic pockets? What replies will your students give?

One enjoyable and enlightening activity is to take a radio and simply start turning the dial. See where the students yell out "stop" or "that's a good station." Discuss why it is good; what makes it current; do they play the latest or just the best? Do students quibble over where the dial should come to rest? Some lively debates develop!

NEW TELEVISION THEMES

Grades: 2 - 8

Materials: Television guides, cassette recorder and cassettes.

Concept:

Listening skills can be developed by testing knowledge of television programs' musical themes.

Activities
&
Directions

Shortly before the start of the school year, new television series make their debuts. An enjoyable activity is having students list their favorites. This can be done in one of several ways:

1. A list is made on the chalkboard.
2. Students make lists on paper at their seats.
3. Television guides are brought to school and favorite programs are circled or underlined.

Once these lists are prepared, other activities can emerge from them. The teacher can take them home. You might want to watch the programs; or, you can even record the television themes on cassette cartridges and bring them to school. Students can thus listen and identify the music. Some teachers make it an informal listening experience. Others turn it into more of a quiz to see how many themes can be identified correctly. We have seen pupils become very excited by the fun of this experience. They feel that the teacher is really "with it" and "knows what's happening." Moreover, listening skills are being developed. Children are discriminating among themes that are now more abstract because the visual associations are eliminated. It is an experience that will lay the groundwork for more sophisticated activities involving jazz, music of Broadway shows, light classics, and classical music.

Creativity
and Humor

Creativity can be fun! Put aside the image of the starving tubercular artist of the nineteenth century; the romantic nonsense that one must suffer to be creative. Think instead of composers and their lighter sides: Mozart's comic operas; Haydn's musical jokes; Schubert's making fun of his own compositions with a kazoo!

Think also of how creative your students can be when you let them. This chapter will try to put that creativity to work in the area of humor—one of the areas students like best.

Here are ideas for comedy, limericks, sketches, slapstick, jokes, dialogue, vaudeville, games, gags, puppets or marionettes, and silent movies—all of which you and your students could have created.

As Beethoven and Schubert poked fun at themselves, you and your students can have fun with music.

JOKES AND RIDDLES

Grades: K - 6

Materials: Books of jokes and riddles.

Concept:

Musical facts can be learned through humorous experiences.

Activities
&
Directions

Question: What musical instrument has an honorary degree conferred upon it?

Answer: Fiddle D. D.

Question: What kind of a bell never asks questions yet requires many answers?

Answer: The doorbell.

You might also have your students try their hand at writing some of their own material. You can start with corny ideas such as:

Question: Did you know that a ski composed music once?

Answer: No

Questioner: Sure, the 1812 Overture was written by Tchaikov-ski.

———————————

Question: What is the keynote of good manners?

Answer: I don't know.

Questioner: B natural!

Some teachers make up riddles with instruments and composers.

Do you know how to get a hot hand in music?

You place the HAND-el in the Beeth-OVEN!

Other riddles can be made up by students, using expressions or phrases such as,

"Why is. . ."

"Why are two. . ."

"When is a. . ."

"When can you. . ."

"What kind of a. . ."

"Why was _____so sad when. . ."

"What's the difference between. . .

"Why can't you. . ."

"If you cross a_____with a _____, what do you get?"

"What happens when. . ."

GAGS AND SKETCHES

Other types of jokes are those of the so-called "stand up comic" who sometimes uses music for his humor. Many of these gags, as they are called, date back to vaudeville and burlesque days where the comic would turn to the band and try to "get their goat." Start with the following lesson, and, if the students start complaining about the material, ask them to bring the gags and sketches up to date. In the process, they will be learning old expressions, even as they snicker.

PLAYING VAUDEVILLE OR BURLESQUE COMICS

Grades: 3 - 8

Materials: Balloon; any old instruments you can find in cellars, attics, etc.

Activities
    &
Directions

Different students act as the different comics; several others act as the band; others act as the accordion player or singer; the remaining students are the audience.

Sketch #1	Comic alone to audience:	Am I a musician? I happen to be a virtuoso of the leaky balloon. (Blows up balloon and makes squeeky noises).
Sketch #2	Accordionist:	Plays real or imaginary accordion.
	Comic:	(Gives the accordion player a funny look, then looks at the audience): Did you ever notice that most accordion players look like they're trying to fold up a road map?
Sketch #3	Singer:	Makes believe he is singing, then gets off stage.
	Comic:	Say, you really have an ear for music. Too bad you don't have a throat for it.
Sketch #4	Comic alone to audience:	(Plays or makes believe he is playing something.) This instrument happens to be 110 years old. I know, my wife made it.
Sketch #5	Band:	(Finishes playing)
	Comic:	(Looks at the band, then turns to the audience.) Isn't it wonderful? These boys

learned all their music from a correspondence course. Let's face it. They must have lost a lot of mail.

Sketch #6	Band:	(Finishes playing.)
	Comic.	Let's face it. Dis band ought to disband.
Sketch #7	Band:	(Finishes playing.)
	Comic:	This is the only band where the drummer carries the melody.
Sketch #8	Band:	(Finishes playing.)
	Comic:	That was _____ and his ragtime band. If you don't believe me, just look at their clothes.
Sketch #9	Comic alone:	(Puts on "bop" outfit—dark glasses and a beret—then puts on what is a "bop" record and starts to snap his fingers and "bop" up and down.) Turns to the audience and says: There's only one trouble with a "bop" record. How can you tell when it is cracked?

The nice thing about all of these sketches is that you can use different students for each one and many different students can get the opportunity to perform. You can also use puppets and marionettes.

Notice, too, how many different aspects of music there are—aspects of music about which the students may ask you such as the accordion, ragtime, and bop music. (In answer to such questions, you might tell them that the accordion uses buttons for chords and bass notes, and uses either a piano keyboard or buttons for the melody depending upon what country the accordion was made in; ragtime was an early form of syncopated music that led to jazz; bop was popular in the late 40's and early 50's.)

ONE-LINERS AND ROUTINES

In vaudeville or burlesque there are also "one-liners"; the comic comes out to an audience and just reels off his material:

Comic:	(Comes onstage, sits down on the piano keys.) That's funny. I usually play by ear!
Comic:	I've played the piano for years—on and off (sits down on the piano stool and falls off). I've got a very slippery stool.

Many of these routines border on the slapstick. Know your pupils, of course, and their parents. If you feel that any of this material will be considered inappropriate, modify it to suit the students with whom you are working. We don't want to offend anyone in the process of making music fun.

One student submitted the following riddle that can be extended for a routine:

Question: In what famous painting does a woman have a musical son?

Answer: *Whistler's Mother*

You might want to explain that the man was not a whistler—one who whistled. It is curious, however, that James Abbott McNeill Whistler was a painter who was very interested in musical ideas and images. We have used the following lesson plan and it works very well.

ECCENTRIC ARTIST ROUTINE

Grades: 4 - 8

Materials: Examples of Whistler's paintings, such as *Harmony in Yellow and Gold*, and *At the Piano*; recording of "I Whistle a Happy Tune" from the broadway musical *The King and I*, or "Whistle While You Work," from the Walt Disney movie *Snow White and the Seven Dwarfs*.

Concepts:

1. Whistler was a 19th century painter who gave musical sounding titles to his paintings.

2. *Whistler's Mother* is a portrait of a mother done by her son. The painting is well known for its interesting composition. (The actual title of the painting is *Arrangement in Gray and Black*.)

Activities
&
Directions

Students enjoy finding berets and finding or making smocks and palettes; brushes are easy enough to get, of course. Whether you use imaginary canvas and easels, or borrow them from the art department, is up to you and your pupils. The object, then, is to enact a scene in which a painter is painting his mother's portrait. For younger children, Whistler can actually *whistle while he works.* But for older pupils, dialogue can be written that could be very funny. Whistler, in the imaginary version, can have a complaining mother who is trying her best to make him feel guilty.

Whistler's Mother:	I'm sitting here for ten hours already. Is this any way to treat a mother?
Whistler:	(Just paints and whistles.)
Whistler's Mother:	Son, I'm talking to you. Why do you treat me this way?
Whistler:	Oh mother, sit still and be quiet!
Whistler's Mother:	See—sacrifice all of your life and this is the way they treat you.
Whistler:	(Moves her slightly and then goes back to whistling and painting.)

. . . . optional . . . in the middle of painting, he stops, puts down his brush, and starts practicing an imaginary musical instrument. . . .

Whistler's Mother:	I'm supposed to sit in this cramped position while you practice that darned _____ .
Whistler:	But mother, music is for relaxation and I need to relax. Besides, you will go down in history!

Try your hand at completing this scene of writing another one. You will see how much fun it is, and how fascinating it can be.

The scene can be made more or less musical, of course. To become more musical, other students can come in while he is working and sit down to play a quartet or trio. With younger students, you might even want to have a parade start to go by while he is trying to paint his mother. And, while she is greatly annoyed, he takes time out to watch the parade!

Have fun!

MUSICAL LIMERICKS

Grades: 2 - 6

Concept:

Creativity can be fostered and developed.

Limericks have always been fun. We're sure that you knew many when you were a child. But, when was the last time you made up any? And, do you use them in the classroom? We'll give you a chance to do both. Here are some musical limericks that we made up and left incomplete. Try completing some yourself. Try having your students complete others. Finally, write some yourself—either alone or as a group project with your class. Don't worry. We feel that yours cannot be worse than ours. In fact, when we use them we call it SMILE time, SMILE standing for:

S illy
M usical
I diomatic
L imericks
E njoyed

**Activities
&
Directions**

Complete these limericks:

*A very old man with a cello
Enjoyed eating ice cream and jello
So C, G, A, E
The four strings, you see
  (to be completed here)* _____

*There was a musician from Kent
Whose saxophone got very bent
'Til one day in June
He played so out of tune
(to be completed here)* _____

*A silly young man with a trumpet
Had tea with just one tiny crumpet
So when supper came,
It was not just a game
  (to be completed here)* _____

*A trombone, a kazoo, and a flute,
Tried using a big parachute
But when halfway down
From the plane, they did frown
  (to be completed here)* _____

*There was a fine sailor from Wales
Who on his ship played piano scales
But one day aboard,
He played the wrong chord
  (to be completed here)* _____

*A lady from Boston played oboe
Her husband was worse than a hobo
So one day instead
Of her going to bed
  (to be completed here)* _____

You can see that there are many musical concepts that can be learned painlessly, using limericks: (1) to spell cello; (2) that the cello has four strings; (3) that there's a *pet* in trumpet; (4) that scales are on the piano as well as on fish; (5) that the piano can play a chord; (6) that an instrument can be "out of tune"; (7) that oboe has a "e" in it but rhymes with hobo. (Is it silly to ask students: "If a dog is a pet, and a cat is a pet, what is a trum-pet?")

Some limericks-to-be-completed can be more personal:

> *I once had two old clarinets*
> *That I used to play for my pets*
> *But doggy got mad*
> *And kitty got scared*
> *(So we put them out and got trum—pets?)*

Other limericks-to-be-completed can be more representative of people than of instruments (as in "The Owl and the Pussy Cat"):

> *A violin, French horn and drum*
> *Made friends with a fun-loving bum*
> *The road they went down*
> *Was the wrong way from town*
>   *(to be completed here)*
>   _____

Here are some additional techniques in a lesson plan format.

MUSICAL LIMERICKS #1

Grades: K - 5

Materials: Books of limericks; books of instruments; pictures of instruments.

Concept:

Limericks can be used in the process of having fun with music.

Activities
    &
Directions

1. With kindergarten children you might not be able to do much more than have the children recite after you. But, one never knows! Sometimes there are very talented youngsters who are capable of completing limericks and/or making up new ones.

2. Children who are beginning to read find limericks fun. The rhyme scheme actually helps students learn pronunciation:

cello — jello	Wales — scales
oboe — hobo	drum — bum
trumpet — crumpet	chord — aboard

Why not try using limericks instead of "See Johnny run"?

MUSICAL LIMERICKS #2

Grades: 5 - 8

Materials: Books and/or encyclopedias on the history of England (or Great Britain); books and pictures of instruments, and the history of musical instruments; map of Great Britain.

Concept:

Limericks can be used in the process of having fun with music.

Activities
&
Directions

1. Older children can do research and read about the history of limericks. As a related activity, you might want to locate the city of Limerick on the map. If you're feeling silly and you've taught alliteration, you might place on the chalkboard:

   "LET'S LOCATE LIMERICK"

   A discussion can follow on whether or not the limerick originated in Limerick.

2. Older students are also more capable of writing their own musical limericks. Ideas can be gotten from any books of limericks. Ideas can also be gotten from pictures of instruments and books on the history of instruments. For example, the precursor of the clarinet was the chalumeau (pronounced SHALL-YOO-MO); a good rhymer for LOW or BOW or even TOE! The precurser of the trombone was the *sackbut.*

   > *A pretty young girl with a bow*
   > *Dug up an old chalumeau*
   > *She said, "Gee, I'm a nut*
   > *Like an ancient sackbut*
   > *(Now my new clarinet's got to go?")*

The parentheses, of course, mean one possible way of ending it. There are many others! Try them. It's fun!

HUMOROUS STORIES

*My chief recollections of the show are the
name of the Wizard, Kibosh, which struck me as
inordinately funny at the time . . . But, however
vague my recollections of the details of the
score. . . . It inspired me with a love and
admiration of Victor Herbert's genius that the
years have never lessened.*

*Deems Taylor**

Humor is one of the best friends that we have in the classroom. And, as pointed out by Deems Taylor, it is one of the "trainers" of the mind. This section presents many humorous stories that you may want to use in introducing music to your students; stories that they will remember for the rest of their lives.

Musical humor is not always something you split your sides laughing over. It generally produces a chuckle, or a smirk, rather than a guffaw. Few people howl—except perhaps other musicians—over a story even as funny as the one about fifty different cello players who were told to meet someone on the very same corner. But, through humor, children can learn many facts about music.

In this section you will find several stories that will probably make you smile. The object will be to tell each one in such a way as to bring out its humor. Set the stage! Paint the backdrop! Make your students feel the comical aspect of the situation. Make them want to act out the stories, to create a farce, to be amused and to want to amuse others—parents or friends. This material can be used for grades 2 – 8.

COPING WITH COPLAND

Aaron Copland, famous American composer, told the story that some-one said: "Oh Mr. Copland, when I hear the ballet *Appalachian Spring*, I can *see* Appalachia and *hear* the spring." The truth of the matter, Mr. Copland recalled, was that when he wrote the ballet for Martha Graham (a major figure in American dance), *he had no idea what the ballet was going to be called!*

In order to make this story funnier, you might make the Copland admirer seem even more foolish by having a high squeaky voice and a gushing mannerism. Mr. Copland, on the other hand, can be made to make the admirer seem silly by giving him spoken dialogue. In other words, have him say: "The *truth* of the matter, *my dear*, is that I had *no* idea what the ballet was going to be called when I wrote it."

---

*© 1945 by Deems Taylor, from *The Well Tempered Listener*. Used by permission of Simon and Schuster Inc., New York.

The scene can be set by having a small cast of characters, let us say, perhaps, Mr. Copland, the Admirer, and an audience or a team of newsmen. Mr. Copland is either giving an address to an audience, or being interviewed by reporters. Your students can make the choice as to which they want it to be.

Another activity can be for your pupils to write a script, elaborating upon this true story to the point where it is barely recognizable. Mr. Copland can be made nicer or meaner; the admirer can be made sillier or more serious. (We ourselves found Mr. Copland extremely nice, by the way, and he probably wasn't at all nasty or sarcastic to the person when the actual incident occurred.)

To obtain more musical details, you might want to assign some of your students to read books about Aaron Copland and Martha Graham. Perhaps, for the younger children, you can read the books yourself, so you can tell the pupils about these two great, creative geniuses. There is also an excellent book on music which Aaron Copland wrote, entitled: *What to Listen For in Music*.

PROUD OF THE PERFECTLY PUNCTUAL PICCOLO PLAYER

A story is told of a conductor who was terribly proud of his piccolo player who never missed a rehearsal. Finally, the conductor decided to give the piccolo player an award for his perfect attendance and punctuality at the next concert. When informed of this fact, he said: "Oh . . . maestro . . . I'm terribly sorry but I can't be at the next concert!"

1. You might want to reenact this scene. Have a group of pupils acting as the orchestra, making believe they are playing. The piccolo player is in the front. The conductor, on a slightly raised platform called a podium (a wooden box will do) is conducting and keeps looking at the piccolo player and smiling. Finally, the conductor stops the musicians and makes his little speech, all the while smiling and being very pleased with both himself and the piccolo player. After the piccolo player's reply, of course, the conductor's smile begins to fade away, becomes a look of embarrassment, and then turns into a scowl.

2. Another musical decision might be whether you have a band or an orchestra. It might be necessary to find seating charts as part of the students' research prior to this activity. Briefly, however, the piccolo player would be in the front if the musical organization was a band (the clarinets being to the conductor's left). In an orchestra, the piccolo player sits in the flute section, which is directly in front of the conductor, behind the viola section.

3. The teacher who contributed this story found that students loved to write the script to accompany the enactment of the scene. The

conductor becomes more and more jubilant in the eyes of some students. For example:

Conductor: Ladies and gentlemen, this is one of the happiest days in my entire career as a conductor . . . etc.

Or, another version:

Conductor: Ladies and gentlemen, tomorrow we will celebrate. In twenty years, Luigi has never missed or been late to one rehearsal or one concert. That is why, tomorrow we are going to celebrate and give him an award . . . etc.

FUNNY STORIES ABOUT CONDUCTORS

The following stories have to do with the traditional animosity and quibbling between conductors and musicians. If you tell them well, your students might even find them uproariously funny.

TALE OF THE TERRIBLE TIMPANIST

This story is about a wealthy amateur musician who had a great ambition to be a famous conductor. So, one day, he hired musicians, formed an orchestra, and started rehearsing the programs. The rehearsal was not going well, and after three hours both the orchestra members and the would-be conductor were getting very irritable. Finally, the timpani player could no longer follow the conductor's beats and came in much too early without a cue, in the middle of a very quiet passage—bang, crash, boom, with a very loud roll on the timpani or kettle drums! Our would-be conductor, in a rage, threw down his baton, glared at the orchestra and, not knowing what happened, demanded, "Now *who* did that?"

This story is so funny because it is hard to imagine even an amateur being that dumb. Of course it borders on the absurd!

In acting out the story, there is probably no need to tell the pupils how to exaggerate. Younger students will readily bang on real or imaginary drums. Spoken dialogue for older pupils can make the amateur conductor overly nice at the beginning, or nasty all the way:

Amateur Conductor: Gentlemen, thank you all so very, very much for
(overly nice)   the wonderfully marvelous opportunity to conduct such fabulously experienced musicians.

Amateur Conductor: Look, I don't want any fooling around here at
(nasty all the way) any time!

You might extend the enactment into a full one-act play in which the amateur musician goes around looking for the musicians who will play in his orchestra. This may lead to questions about the sociology of the whole situation. How *do* you go about starting an orchestra? Where do you get the musicians? How do you audition them? What is an audition? A good project might be calling up or visiting a Musicians' Union and interviewing an officer. Be sure the question is asked, "What is a musical contractor?" (This is especially effective in the upper grades.)

On the other hand, younger students might want to stick to the situation itself, as is, emphasizing the aspect of arguing:

Conductor: You people call yourself professional musicians?

Musician: But maestro, you don't know a downbeat from an upbeat. How are we supposed to follow you?

Conductor: You idiot! That is your problem!!

This type of dialogue can also be improvised, after some terms are defined. *Maestro* is an Italian word for the master of the orchestra or the conductor. It is usually uttered with respect. The *downbeat* is when the conductor's hand literally goes down. The *upbeat*, conversely, is when the conductor's hand comes up.

Notice how many facts and how much understanding can be acquired, all in the spirit of fun. And, you will notice how many musicial gestures are quite naturally part of students' nonverbal vocabularies—perceptions that they have picked up from television or concerts in the park.

LULLY'S LEG

The story of Lully's leg is sort of like laughing at someone who slipped on a banana peel. We probably should not laugh at it. But, teachers for some time have found that students always laugh at the story even when it is told "straight," so, we thought that we might as well tell it as a humorous story.

The tale tells us a great deal about how advanced and sophisticated we are in music. Compared to modern day conducting, one of the old ways seems absurdly crude! Orchestral conducting was not a fine art as it is today. Up until the eighteenth century, some conductors would keep time by banging on the floor with a large wooden stick, to try to keep the orchestra together. One of these conductors was also a famous French composer, Jean Baptiste Lully. And, it is written that, one day, while keeping time with such a device, he hit his foot accidentally. Infection set in and he died as a result. As we said, it is not really funny, but, students laugh whether you want them to or not (as they are learning about the evolution of modern conducting).

The possibilities for pantomime, or for spoken dialogue, are enormous. First of all, the children will love to use the French accent.

Lully: (spoken with a fake French accent)	Gentlemen, gentlemen! Please stay in time, I am banging out the beat as hard as I can. Do you want me to get a heart attack?

Or,

Lully:	No, No, no, no! But of course you know that *zees ees not corrrrrect!!*

Or,

Lully:	I have tried to explain to you *zo meny tams*, I bang *zee beat forrrr yeuh* to *hearrrreet!!!!*

A proper funeral and burial, of course, can also be added to this minia-ture play. Some teachers then experiment with a baton, the conductor's stick that, in modern days, is supposed to keep the orchestra together. Can you use it? (Read, or re-read Chapter 3 on conducting gestures.) You and your students will probably have a lot of fun trying to use it correctly. (Exactly how to hold it varies, even among professional conductors, so don't worry about it.)

PLAY THOSE RESTS!

Grade Level: 3 - 8

Materials: Stencils or rexograph-masters; a musical *score* (not essential); music stand (not essential).

Concept:

1. A *rest* in music means you don't play for a specified number of counts or beats. See Figure 2.

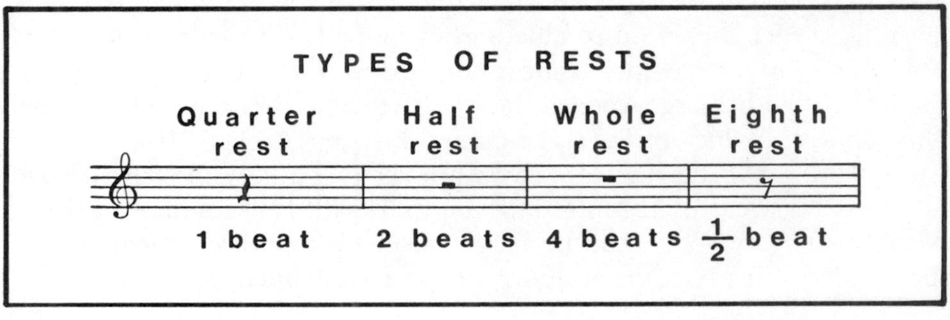

```
              TYPES   OF   RESTS

      Quarter      Half      Whole     Eighth
       rest        rest      rest       rest

    1 beat     2 beats   4 beats   ½ beat
```

Figure 2

2. The *pit* is where you place an orchestra for a musical play or opera.

3. A *score* is prepared by a composer and contains all the music and lyrics of a musical play; there are also *scores* for symphonies and ballets, etc.

Story:* Shubert the producer (the Shubert theatre in New York bears his name), in a bad mood from a fracas with an actor, advanced toward the orchestra pit and pointed at the second violinist. "What's the matter with that man," he demanded of the conductor, "Why wasn't he playing just now?"

The tall dignified composer and arranger of the music was wielding the baton himself in the exigencies of dress rehearsal. He blinked at Mr. Shubert uncertainly. "But his part calls for a twelve-bar rest at this point. There's nothing written for him in the score." Shubert the producer replied, still snarling, "Then write him something—I pay him a good salary!"

**Activities
&
Directions**

1. Type up or duplicate this dialogue. Then reenact the scene, using a mock play and an orchestra pit. In other words, there are many parts for extras in the old Hollywood sense. As many as seven to ten students can be doing pantomime in the imaginary musical play that is taking place. As many as fifteen to twenty pupils can be pantomiming the movements of an orchestra. Then, the two principals playing Shubert and the conductor start their little dialogue. You might also write an extra line or two for the second violinist whose reactions we can imagine. He can be shocked, angry, amused, incensed, or unflustered. You take your pick, or have the students improvise their parts.

2. Students with artistic talent can draw or paint this scene. We have had some very interesting results. Shubert can be onstage, glaring down at the second violinist and conductor in the pit. Another version might have Shubert hovering in a menacing fashion right over the second violinist.

3. You might want to place Figure 2 on the chalkboard and explain rests to your pupils. It is really quite simple. A note means that you play your instrument. A *rest* means that you don't play. How long you play or how long you rest is determined by the symbol that is used. Clap your hands in steady beats. If you stopped for one of those counts, that stopping would be represented by a one-beat rest. If you

---

*Cited in *The Time of Laughter* (Little Brown and Co.), p. 144. © 1967, Corey Ford. Used by permission from the Estate of Corey Ford.

stopped for two beats, those two beats would have been represented by a two-beat rest. Four beats of silence is represented by a four-beat rest.

Fun with Movement

Most things move. Much has been written about movement in nature—the regular ebb and flow of the tides, the changing of the seasons, day and night, the falling rain and snowflakes. But it is the regular, recurring patterns of beats and accents that make for the phenomenon known as music. "Music makes me want to dance," is one cliché. "Music helps me relax and get to sleep," is another. The merry-go-round is accompanied by a very hypnotic beat. We cannot see a merry-go-round move without thinking of its music. Instrumentalists move when they play, and the conductor moves in a different way as he conducts them. Ballroom, tap, and ballet dancers all move in different ways to music. The chorus moves in a particular way to get onstage, sings and then gets off. Children jumping rope move in still other ways as they move to their own vocal or clapped rhythms. Circus performers move in their distinct ways with music heightening or punctuating tensions. Marching bands and cheerleaders have carefully worked out patterns of moving through space and time. You can probably think of several more unique movements that have their basis in music or would not be the same without it.

In this chapter, we will explore movement in music. And there is very little that we have mentioned—circus performers, the merry-go-round, cheerleading, jumping rope, dancing—that is not fun. So why not make musical movement fun? (Dancing is such a favorite pastime of so many people that we have made a separate chapter on music and dance.) Here are activities for you to use and have many enjoyable hours exploring the ways in which music and movement are inextricably interwoven.

NAME GAME*

Grades: 1 - 6

Materials: Recording of Symphony No. 5 in C Minor, Op. 67 by Beethoven; recording of and/or music for "Twinkle, Twinkle Little Star," "America," "Happy Birthday to You," and "The Star-Spangled Banner."

Concepts:

1. Names can be associated with musical rhythms.
2. Learning musical rhythms can be fun.
3. Musical memory can be improved.

Activities
&
Directions

This is an excellent activity to use in September for learning other students' names. In this game everyone stands around in a circle. One pupil starts. Each child gives his or her name and then claps, snaps, or taps a rhythm. The idea is to remember one's own rhythm as well as those of others, in addition to their names. It is easier than you think. When we give some examples, you will see how you actually hear the rhythms in your mind.

Student	Rhythm
#1	rhythm of opening theme of Symphony No. 5 in C Minor by Beethoven
#2	rhythm of "Twinkle, Twinkle, Little Star"
#3	rhythm of "America" ("My Country 'Tis of Thee")
#4	rhythm of "Happy Birthday" and/or "The Star-Spangled Banner"

1. After everyone gives his/her rhythm, the first pupil starts again. The object is to give one's own rhythm, name, and then clap, snap, or tap someone else's. The pupil whose rhythm has been remembered then steps out to the center and tries to remember still another rhythm. So on and so forth. You may not believe this but the first time or two the game is played, students will not remember their own rhythms!

---

*Our thanks to Kathy, Dan, and Robert of the Lincoln Center Institute, Lincoln Center of New York City, for the basic idea of this game. The game was played in the summer of 1979, using creative dance movements. (Permission to use granted by Mark Schubart, Director, Lincoln Center Institute.)

2. Another way the game can be played is with touching and then making a noise. For example, if you were "it," you would touch me and make a noise. You must remember your own noise. I then touch another person and make a different noise. That person continues the game with yet another noise, and so on and so forth. Some examples are as follows.

Student	Noise
#1	whistle
#2	grunt
#3	sigh
#4	click
#5	pop
#6	suck
#7	cry
#8	whine
#9	moo (cow)
#10	meow (cat)
#11	bark (dog)
#12	crow (rooster)
#13	baa (sheep)
#14	cluck, cluck

You can see that once you get into animal sounds, the possibilities are almost endless. Your students should be able to think of many that we omitted. The same is true of the "mouth sounds" that we started with. There are many sounds that can be made with the mouth but are difficult to describe on paper.

We've included this lesson in this chapter on fun with movement because the basic thrust is getting into a circle, touching another student, and then making a noise. Movement is its basis. But, naturally, you can see that a musical composition can be made out of these sounds and even recorded.

DISCO DANCING

Grades: 2 - 8

Materials: Several tape recorders (cassette and/or reel to reel); one or two record players; flashing lights if you can obtain them.

Concepts:

1. As with other popular music before it, disco borrowed freely from the classics.

2. Students have fun being recording engineers and working with musical equipment.

Activities
&
Directions

1. Disco dancing—the rage, the craze of the late 70's. You can teach it to children (if they are young enough), or they can teach it to you (if they are old enough). One teacher we know sets up her room like a real discotheque, flashing lights and all! You might want to use several tape recorders and/or record players so you can start one record before the other stops as in a real discothèque.

2. This activity is included in this chapter for one simple reason (rather than in the chapter called "Fun Dances"). Discothèque was meant to be a total experience. Although there are specific steps, the process of recordings merging in and out of each other is as important as the specific steps done. Many people just move creatively, doing their own choreography. The disc jockey is like the conductor of an orchestra.

3. *Saturday Night Fever* was one of the first movies to portray the disco craze. Try to see how much your students know about this movie. Their knowledge of the music might surprise you. There were some "classics" in the film also, such as the disco versions of Beethoven's Fifth Symphony ("A Fifth of Beethoven") and Mussorgsky's *A Night on Bald Mountain.*

ROLLER DERBY—DISCO ON WHEELS

Grades: 2 - 8

Materials: Roller skates.

Activities
&
Directions

As with the last lesson on disco dancing, the same materials, concepts, and activities can be used with the addition of another dimension—wheels. Roller skating has long been fun for children. But only in the late '70's did "disco on wheels" become a craze. Roller skating to disco music makes the roller skating different of course.

One admonition. Be careful! Your principal's permission is needed, quite naturally. But if he or she is agreeable, you'll be in for a lot of fun!! A gymnasium is probably preferable to a classroom, but if chairs and desks are movable, a disco on wheels lesson can take place in the classroom also.

ICE SKATING TO MUSIC

Grades: 2 - 8

Materials: Ice skates; transistor radios or portable record player.

Activities
&
Directions

Another movement activity is ice skating to music. We doubt if your principal will permit dry ice to be brought into the school, so this activity involves something of a trip. It may be out to the local pond or lake if there is one nearby. All precautions should be taken to follow local ordinances. Be sure to check with an assistant or vice principal on particulars.

If the activity is approved, transistor radios and/or transistorized record players can be used.

1. Try doing disco on ice. It might be novel.
2. Using such old standards as the "Skater's Waltz," a traditional approach can be taken in which one tries for lyric grace and beauty of movement.
3. Including only the excellent skaters, try using some ballet movements. There have been some beautiful television skating pageants, precluding the need to show a film of what you mean. However, you might want to obtain such a film. Check with your librarian or audio-visual coordinator.

MOVING LIKE MUSIC

Grades: K - 6

Concepts:

1. Music goes up in pitch (ascends) and down in pitch (descends).
2. Music gets faster and slower (accelerates and decelerates).
3. Music gets louder and softer (dynamics).

Activities
&
Directions

1. Place on the chalkboard:

   AIM: TO MOVE LIKE MUSIC

   Ask your students if they can "move like music." See if they can discover for themselves that music goes higher or lower, gets faster and slower, and gets louder and softer. Can they make any other discoveries? We have found that pupils are often very surprising!

2. Musical tones going up and down the scale can be explored with a simple game. All that is needed is for the students to wear old clothing or clothing they don't mind getting dirty. (Make sure to notify parents and/or obtain your principal's consent.)

Up the Scale	Down the Scale
A – students are lying down	G – standing and stretching (on chair)
B – students sit up	F – just standing on a chair
C – sit on chair	E – standing and stretching (on floor)
D – students stand	D – just standing
E – students stretch	C – sitting on chair
F – stand on chair	B – sitting on floor
G – stretch hands while standing on chair	A – lying on floor

   We have made "Up the Scale" the notes ABCDEFG, so you could use resonator bells or a song flute, or a piano, if you have them. Any scale can be used. If you do not know the notes on the piano, any seven different keys can be used. So-called Swiss *Melode Bells* are very reasonable in price and use the scale F, G, A, Bflat, C, D, and E.

3. Students quickly learn the concept of tempo. "There are slow dances and fast dances," they have told us. So it is, too, with loud and soft music, although they sometimes confuse loud with fast.

Concept: Music gets faster and slower.

Ask students to make believe they are conductors. Have them make the music go faster and faster. Can they do it? Do they look like they are having fun? Most teachers reported that to their students "fast was fun." Don't be upset, by the way, when your students call slow music "boring." They merely have not yet added to their vocabulary such words as melancholy, dreary, pensive, sad, etc.

Concept: Music gets louder and softer.

Ask your new "conductors" to make their imaginary orchestras get louder and louder. How will they start moving their hands? Will their fingers be doing anything interesting? The Italian word for getting louder and louder is *crescendo* (CRE-SHEN-DO). Getting softer is *diminuendo* (DIMIN-YOU-ENDO).

CONDUCTING 2/4

Grades: 3 - 8

Materials: Batons or sticks of wood that look like a conductor's baton (not essential); music stands (not essential).

Concepts:

1. 2/4 is called a *meter sign* which tells you that beats or accents are grouped in two.
2. A *polka* is one dance that is often in 2/4 meter.

Activities
&
Directions

1. A polka is a fun dance. Did you know that it often uses a musical meter sign of 2/4? You might place Figure 3 on the chalkboard and explain to your students that you then count ONE two, ONE two, ONE two; accenting one and grouping beats in twos. Common polkas can then be played or sung as you dance (for example, "Too Fat Polka," or "Beer Barrel Polka").

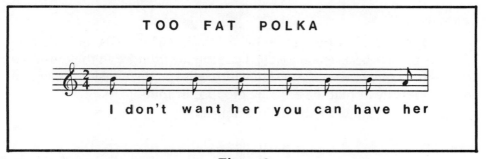

TOO   FAT   POLKA

I don't want her you can have her

Figure 3

2. The students who are not dancing (are there any who *are* dancing?) can stand around the room that has been cleared of desks and chairs. They can practice the very simple pattern for conducting 2/4 time or

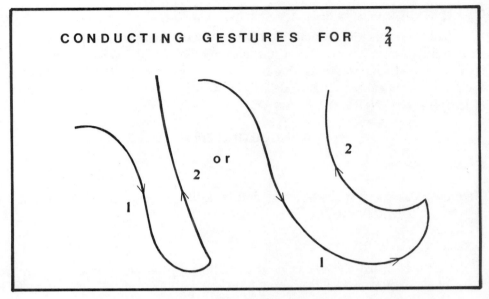

CONDUCTING GESTURES FOR $\frac{2}{4}$

or

2

1

2

2

1

1

Figure 4

meter (see Figure 4). They can use real or fake batons, or, no batons at all. The hand will do.

3/4 AND 4/4 TIME

Grades: 3 - 7

Materials: Batons or sticks of wood that look like a conductor's baton (not essential); music stands (not essential); pictures of people at a ball where a waltz is being performed in the ballroom.

Concepts:

1. 3/4 is called a *time signature* or *meter sign* which tells you that there are three beats in a measure; i.e., beats are grouped in three. 4/4 is a *time signature* or *meter* sign which tells you there are four beats in a measure or that the beats are grouped by fours.
2. A *waltz* is a dance that is in 3/4 meter.

Activities
&
Directions

1. A waltz is one of the most colorful dances as well as being fun to do. Pretty young girls often love to dress up as if they were at a fancy ball

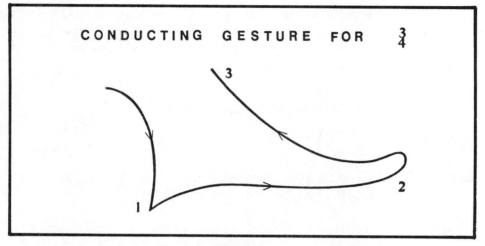

Figure 5

doing the waltz. You might get this concept across by showing pictures of dancers doing the waltz with long, flowing skirts. Do you and your students know that a waltz is in 3/4 or three quarter time? The beat can be felt best by going OOM pah pah, OOM pah pah, or ONE two three, ONE two three, ONE two three. Place Figure 5 on the chalkboard and, with your students, try to feel the beat of ONE two three, ONE two three. Try to explain the concept of how beats are grouped in threes with an accent being placed on the first beat: *OOM* pah pah.

2. *Common time* is another name for 4/4 time. When Figure 6 is seen at the beginning of music, it means that beats are grouped in fours, a very common occurrence in music. Since this large "C" on a music staff is so simple to make, it is fun to do. Children love simplicity and repetition. If your pupils are agreeable, practice drawing this symbol for 4/4 time or meter. If this does not offer opportunity for enough movement, marching around the room can be another activity. Not all marches are written in 4/4 or *common time*. But enough are, to help give 4/4 its nickname. To drive home the concept, marching

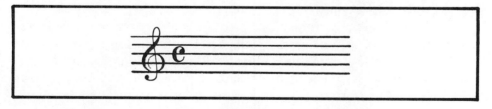

Figure 6

should be done with the recitation of ONE two three four, ONE two three four, ONE two three four. We should not presume that all children automatically know this, nor that all teachers are aware of this elemental fact.

RAGTIME RHYTHM

Grades: 4 - 8

Materials: Books about ragtime; pictures and recordings; music for the movie *The Sting* ("The Entertainer" by Scott Joplin).

Concepts:

1. Sometimes considered pre-jazz and other times considered early jazz, ragtime is highly *syncopated* music in which accents come between beats or on beats not normally accented.
2. The movie *The Sting* used music by Scott Joplin, a black American composer of rags and ragtime.

**Activities
&
Directions**

1. Stomping and clapping can be taught easily enough, don't you think? Just alternate FOOT hand, FOOT hand, FOOT hand, etc. But then try to count as this is done: ONE and, TWO and, THREE and, FOUR and. The "and" is squeezed in between the beats. This is easy enough and is done in any march. More difficult, however, is to *emphasize* or accent the "and" instead of the beat. For example, One AND, two AND, three AND, four AND. This is the essence of ragtime, emphasizing the "off beats." Try going back to the alternation of feet and hands and do the following: make the hand clap much louder and a little longer than before (foot HAND . . ., foot HAND . . . , foot HAND . . . , foot HAND . . . one AND, two AND, three AND, four AND).
2. Using books, recordings, and pictures, students might further investigate the music of ragtime—where it came from, how it got its name, what a *rag* is, who Scott Joplin was. Recorded examples can be used. The greatest rags are considered to be those of Scott Joplin, a great black American composer. Discussion can center around the movie *The Sting* which returns to local theatres periodically, as well as

television. Students can practice movements as well as dress and designing scenery. Older students can be directors and producers, younger pupils can be the actors and ragtime pianists. (Until they were recently orchestrated, all ragtime music was for the piano.) Other great ragtime pianists were Eubie Blake and Willie (the lion) Smith.

BOP BEATS

Grades: 1 - 8

Materials: Berets; dark glasses; any other articles of clothing that might be associated with the bop or be-bop era; recordings by Charlie Parker and Dizzy Gillespie (such as Dizzy Gillespie's "I'm Boppin Too").

Activities
&
Directions

As with ragtime, you and your students can have fun with movement using the type of jazz known as *be-bop* or *bop*. The first movement to learn is bobbing the head up and down while some Charlie Parker recordings are being played. Do it with "shades" (dark glasses) and berets, and the "scene" will be completed—man! Additional fun can be had by snapping the fingers at various times, and exclaiming "yeah man, yeah!" We have found that this fun can be the basis for music lessons dealing with that period. Students may bring in books about the period: about the great black musicians like Charlie Parker, Dizzy Gillespie, and Kenny "Klook" Clark; about the beginnings of *bop* in Harlem's Minton's Nightclub. Maps of New York City may be used to locate Harlem in Manhattan. (Another fun bop activity can be found in *Elementary Teacher's Music Almanack,* by the authors, Parker Publishing Company.)

SNAPPING, CLAPPING, AND TAPPING

Grades: K - 2

Materials: Recording of or music for "He's Got the Whole World in His Hands."

Concept:

Clapping helps students learn to keep the beat.

Activities
&
Directions

1. Before the second or third grade, most students cannot "snap" their fingers. But they sure get a kick out of *your* doing it! In fact, they are usually quite fascinated with anyone who can snap his fingers—especially if you do it loud. It is a great deal of fun for the teacher and pupils alike to go through the process of learning this skill. Be prepared for much physical contact as the children try to discover what it is you do to get the "snap." They will examine all of your fingers but especially the thumb. This activity, of course, sets the stage for all the finger-snapping activities of working with rhythms. It is basic to many musical movements. One of the recordings that many teachers use for this activity is "Something's Coming" from Leonard Bernstein's *West Side Story* (lyrics by Stephen Sondheim). Children love to try to imitate the opening of the song: "Cool (*snap*) Cool (*snap*) . . ."

2. Tapping and clapping are other musical movements. We often see children tapping on desks and, all too often, the "offenders" are asked to stop. You won't stop them, will you? After all, they are only exploring rhythms and beats that they "feel" or hear "in their head." In fact, during some work breaks you might try (as other teachers are beginning to do) to "join 'em" instead of trying to "beat 'em." Let the more musical students get some excess energy out of their systems by tapping on the desk. All you need is a sympathetic, music-loving school principal and—perhaps—some earplugs or a transistor radio with an ear jack. Have fun!

3. Clapping is easy, right? For you, yes; but not for all children. Using an easy song that most people know, such as "He's Got the Whole World in His Hands," watch how many of your pupils will clap completely out of rhythm. If you are very musical, you will be able to spot it right away (and probably understand *exactly* what we mean when we say "try to get the children to clap on the off beat"). What we mean is, you can clap on ONE and THREE, *or*, TWO and FOUR. Try counting ONE two THREE four, ONE two THREE four. Now reverse it: one TWO three FOUR, one TWO three FOUR. Continue the game as below.

	Counting	Clapping
First way:	ONE two THREE four	CLAP two CLAP four
Second way:	one TWO three FOUR	one CLAP three CLAP

BASIC BALLET

Grades: K - 8

Materials: Pictures of ballet dancers; recordings of well-known ballet music such as Tchaikovsky's *Nutcracker Suite* or *Swan Lake*.

Concepts:

1. A *ballerina* is a female ballet dancer.
2. *Ballet*, originating in France, is a very stylized form of dancing to music.

Activities
&
Directions

1. Place on the chalkboard:

   BASICALLY BALLET

   See if the alliteration of "BASICALLY BALLET" can stimulate any word associations (such as "MOSTLY MOZART"). Older students can then be asked if they know what ballet is. Discussion can be mixed with showing pictures of male and female ballet dancers. Young teen-agers often think that all male ballet dancers are effeminate and snicker when asked about it. This misconception and prejudice must be broken down. The question is how? Our ballet-dancing friends and colleagues have told us that it has to be done in two ways. One is through having live, very robust and masculine male dancers visit schools. The second way is through using the term *creative movement*—never using the word *ballet*—and only later on making the association. It helps, also, if one of your students (or several) takes ballet lessons. Another enjoyable activity is to see a live ballet such as *Swan Lake* or *The Nutcracker*. The creative movement that you use can be almost anything—you do not have to be very musical! Impressionistic movement of any sort contributes to an understanding of what it is that dancers do. Upper graders are also capable of doing research to learn about the development of ballet in France.
2. Younger children have fewer preconceived notions and prejudices. You might be able to get them to assume the poses of the dancers in whatever pictures you use—without any laughter but with a great deal of genuine fun and enjoyment. It is those poses that are some-

times the essence of creative movement, not the more sophisticated choreography that very few people and even very few dancers ever get to understand completely. Once the poses are assumed, the children can use whatever movements they want to go from one pose to another. Walking, running, jumping, leaping, playing basketball, soccer, football, hockey, skipping, and hopping can all be used. Be sure to include the activity of clipping out pictures of fighters and ballplayers in action—to get even more ideas of creative movements and body poses.

The ballet position of, let us say, the left heel touching the arch of the right foot, is also something that is easy to teach. You might ask, "is this ballet?" The answer is, "Yes, basic ballet."

GETTING GOSPEL

Grades: 2 - 8

Materials: Any books or articles on gospel music; recordings by black gospel singers such as Mahalia Jackson (including such songs as "He's Got the Whole World in His Hands," "Just a Closer Walk with Thee," "Nearer My God to Thee," and "Move on Up a Little Higher"; pictures of Mahalia Jackson, or of current gospel singers, or of a church you know of where gospel music is sung; recordings of Broadway musicals that feature gospel music such as *Your Arms Too Short to Box with God*; tambourines.

Concept:

One aspect of the black experience is gospel music; Mahalia Jackson, born in 1911 in New Orleans (like Louis Armstrong), was a black vocalist well known for singing gospel music.

Activities
&
Directions

1. What movements are associated with gospel? What first comes to mind—the "off-beat" hand clap (one TWO three FOUR, one CLAP three CLAP), the use of tambourines, the shaking hands held high over the head, or the moving head and marching around while the body does "bow-like" movements? Perhaps all of them? We have

seen many pupils having lots of fun while imitating parents (or the older folks) having a gospel experience. If you cannot immediately envision what we have just described, you might want to obtain books, films, and pictures about gospel music. If you have seen renditions and performances of gospel music, then you know exactly what we have described and more. Many music teachers play the part of a gospel preacher who calls for exclamations such as "yes," "I feel it," "Uh huh," "mm hmm," etc. (One caution; check with your principal and parents to make sure there are no objections to what some may think is a violation of separation of church and state.)

2. Another enjoyable activity is using tambourines. With younger children, a simple exploratory experience might be enough. With older pupils, you might be very pleasantly surprised to find out that one of your students knows how to do some pretty fancy things with the tambourine. We have heard squeals of enthusiasm when passing out a dozen or so tambourines!

SNAPPY SPIRITUALS

Grades: 2 - 8

Materials: Recordings of spirituals sung by college choirs, Martina Arroyo, Paul Robeson, Leontyne Price, and Marian Anderson.

Concepts:

1. Many spirituals, created by black slaves in the United States to be sung at their religious services, were originally sung à capella (without any instrumental accompaniment).

2. Some spirituals were fast, peppy, or snappy—often ones which sung of "crossing the river" or putting on some magical piece of clothing to transport one to Heaven, e.g., "Good News the Chariot's Coming."

**Activities
&
Directions**

1. In preparation for this lesson, you might first listen to recordings to choose spirituals that are both fast and truly à capella. (In recent years, many spirituals which were originally sung unaccompanied have been arranged with piano and even orchestral accompaniments. Which ones are fast and peppy? Which ones want to make

you get up and shout? Which stimulate rhythmic, musical movements? Try to get the students to move rhythmically in any way that might relate to the concept of spirituals dealing with "flying up to heaven," "getting on the train," "climbing up the ladder," or other distinctive ways of moving.

2. With older students, you might have a general discussion about spirituals and their dealing with biblical passages or the desire to find peace in the afterlife. If you have recordings by Martina Arroyo, Leontyne Price or Marian Anderson, you might want to mention their roles as stars of the Metropolitan Opera in New York City. If you've been able to obtain a recording by Paul Robeson, you may or may not want to relate the tragedy of his being black-listed in the 1930's because he was a communist, and that he eventually went to Russia to live. These are all ideas that work well with intellectually gifted students who are concerned with broad, social issues. Gifted pupils can also choreograph musical movements and have fun doing it. Perhaps some of them are taking modern interpretive dancing in the traditions of Graham, St. Denis, Ailey, Limon, Cunningham, Fosse, Champion etc., and you can discuss modern choreography.

TAMBOURINES, TIMBALES, AND TAMALES

Grades: K - 8

Materials: Tambourine or tambourines; pictures of bulls and bullfights; recordings of the Tijuana Brass; a map of the Caribbean, Latin and South Americas; pictures of timbales (perhaps from a musical instrument catalogue); recordings of *salsa* music by Latin American orchestras from Puerto Rico, or New York.

Concepts:

1. Timbales are Afro-Cuban instruments that are used, now, in most Hispanic and popular music bands.
2. Tambourines, often associated with gospel, are also used in many fundamentalist prayer meetings.

Activities
   &
Directions

1. Tamales rhymes with timbales—so our original impetus is more poetic than musical. But, upon further investigation and consulta-

tion with other professionals, it turns out that we can allude to the music of *tamales territory*. How many styles would love to claim this vast heritage of musical vitality? How many countries would love to be able to claim the same rhythmic vitality and robust movements? Younger children, who love to do the Mexican Hat Dance, will also love the other exciting movements of the bullfight. Fun with movement, in this case, can mean moving like the *toreador* (bullfighter) or like the bull! Bullfight music such as the "Toreador Song" from *Carmen* and/or Tijuana Brass music can be played in the background as your young choreographers decide who is what and who moves where. Teachers have gone so far as to send us scripts of children's dialogues with the usual banter: "I'll be the bull"; "No! I'll be the bull!"; "I'll be the horse"; "No! I'll be the horse!" etc. Correlation with social studies can be provided by using a map to locate Mexico—our southern neighbor. (Additional material on Mexico and music can be found in *Elementary Teacher's Music Almanack*, by the authors, p. 142.)

2. We've had great success with tambourines. So often—perhaps because they are used also in rock and disco—students know exactly how to use them and have fun, sometimes shouting *"Hallelujah"* and sometimes using them in Spanish fashion. You might want to play rock, soul, disco, or any other music that uses a hard afterbeat on TWO and FOUR. Timbales are also fun to use, but few children know how to use them. They are a set of two differently tuned drums on one stand, played with sticks and sometimes the hands also. Tito Puente was a great virtuoso on the timbales, so you can use his records to demonstrate the instrument.

4

Drama, Music, and Fun

Drama comes as naturally to children as does music. They play with toys and dolls. They play cowboys and Indians. They play doctor and nurse. They play railroad engineer. Is it any wonder that drama and music have such a close affinity for them? They make up stories and fit songs to them. We often hear children saying to each other, "You be the _____ " And, of course, the other child replies, "No, I want to be the _____ ." The very next moment they are singing a song appropriate to the action or play-acting. This close affinity of music with drama can be harnessed in the classroom. Although fun with music is our central focus, drama can help combine other arts in addition to music: finger, water, and oil paints (for scenery) for example.

In this chapter you will find ideas for combining the action of drama with the fun aspects of music. What is it about good drama that lends itself so well to musical presentation? Think of all the Shakespeare plays that were later made into musical presentations (*Othello, Romeo and Juliet, Macbeth, Falstaff, A Midsummer Night's Dream*). Throughout the eighteenth and nineteenth centuries, opera was very much the equivalent of our Broadway musical; and *singspiel, opera comique,* and *opera buffa* were very much the equivalent of our musical comedy. Think of how Damon Runyon's zany characters were incorporated into *Guys and Dolls*; how *Anna and the King of Siam* became *The King and I*. All of this material can be used as we look for the links, the essential ingredients of what children do naturally in their play situations and how these ingredients can be incorporated into a slightly more sophisticated excursion into our dramatic-musical heritage.

Figure 7

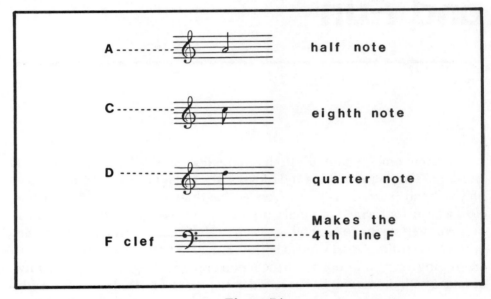

Figure 7A

You might want to use Figure 7 as a wallchart to: (1) usher in this unit of study; or (2) teach musical concepts. For example, can your pupils guess the alphabetical names of the notes that are used instead of letters in "Drama, Music, and Fun?" (Answer: A, C, and D. Moreover, the A is a half note, the C is an eighth note, and the D is a quarter note.) Can your pupils guess that the sign in "Fun" is an F clef?

Let's start off with some scene-making and dramatic energizers. Elaborate upon these lesson plans as you wish.

PAINT YOUR WAGON

Grades: 2 - 8

Materials: Toy wagons; finger paints; crayons; oil colors; oaktag; colored paper; recording of the Broadway show *Paint Your Wagon*.

Concepts:

1. Drama can help relate music and other arts.
2. Broadway musical comedies are a unique American art form.

**Activities
&
Directions**

1. What an opportunity for incorporating finger paint, water colors, oil colors, or even crayons, with music! With the music to *Paint Your Wagon* in the background, perhaps, you can structure an assortment of arts and crafts activities:
   a. painting toy wagons,
   b. making covered wagons out of oaktag,
   c. drawing scenes of covered wagons with water, oil, or finger paints.

   We have merely used the title of the show as a point of departure, of course; but you might want to listen for anything else in the lyrics that will stimulate your class.

2. Younger students love to play "Cowboys and Indians." What better opportunity than an activity with wagons? The pupils can circle the wagons for the inevitable battle. But, of course, older children can dig deeply into the aspect of social injustice and the entire history of our westward expansion. Debates can be structured regarding treatment of the Indian nations during this period. To what extent were the Indian nations treated harshly? Unfairly? Violently? Debates can also be structured regarding the role of women during this period. Were they liberated? Were they second class citizens?

3. Are there any songs you can make up to add to the show? Are there any that you might want to cut out at the present time? Are there any that you would want to update? This could be a good way to start a discussion of the American musical theatre and how it is a uniquely American art form. At this point, we have sometimes played an aria in French or Italian, to draw a comparison with what was a current art form in its day.

OKLAHOMA

Grades: 4 - 8

Materials: A recording of Rodgers and Hammerstein's *Oklahoma*; cowboy and farmer outfits or costumes; hoes and shovels; wood for making a coffin.

Concepts:

    1. Drama can help relate music and industrial arts.

    2. Every decade or so, dancing is revolutionized by a great mind.

Activities
&
Directions

    1. How, you might ask, can building a coffin be fun? Well, believe it or not, children will find the activity amusing. They won't find it depressing at all! In fact, the song "Poor Jud is Dead" was one of the funniest numbers in *Oklahoma*. And, of course, there are few things easier to build than a coffin. After it is made (Halloween might be a good time for the project), it can be sat on, used as a miniature stage for puppets, or used for a picnic table. Listen to the song "Poor Jud is Dead" several times. Picture how you and your class would set this scene. Picture the humor of someone almost being buried without really being dead. Children find it funny. How about you?

    2. Agnes De Mille, a niece of famed Cecil B. De Mille, revolutionized choreography in her dances for the Richard Rodgers music. It is beyond the scope of this book to explain exactly how, but we do know that the experts speak of how Broadway dancing was never again the same afterwards. Once having seen it, either on Broadway or in the movies, one never forgets it—the frolic of "The Cowboys and the Farmers Should be Friends"; or the naturalness of "Oh What a Beautiful Morning"; or the almost naive simplicity of "I'm Just a Girl Who Can't Say No." You might want to discuss other Broadway choreographers such as Bob Fosse or Gower Champion.

    3. So often, on a beautiful clear day, we wake up and immediately think of the song "Oh What a Beautiful Morning." Many songs in *Oklahoma* have the ability to evoke strong imagery and sentiments. Moreover, the entire play lends itself to planning, drawing, and making original scenery. For almost twenty years, we have seen many teachers stage portions of it or the entire work. Have you ever thought of doing it? Here is your chance! You can always play the music and have your pupils do pantomime. Some teachers do it that way.

SOUTH PACIFIC

Grades: 3 - 8

Materials: A map of the world; recording of the Broadway musical *South Pacific*; leis; pictures of Hawaii and/or other South Pacific islands.

Concepts:

1. Hawaii and other South Pacific islands have a unique cultural heritage;
2. The *hula* is one of the fun dances that South Pacific culture has yielded;
3. *South Pacific* is another one of the many famous Broadway musicals that were written by Richard Rodgers and Oscar Hammerstein.

Activities
&
Directions

1. When the novel *Tales of the South Pacific* by James Michener was made into the musical *South Pacific*, by Richard Rodgers and Oscar Hammerstein, it was another landmark in the marriage of great drama and music via literature. Think of the scope of its songs such as "Some Enchanted Evening," "Bali Hai," "Dites-Moi," and "Happy Talk." "Some Enchanted Evening" was originally sung by one of the greatest baritones in the history of the Metropolitan Opera in New York City, Ezio Pinza. "Happy Talk" is an amusing song that also illustrates the Bali style of repeating words. Play the original cast recording and note the richness of Ezio Pinza's operatic voice. You might also discuss his accent, his having been born in Italy. Compare the songs as to the different emotions they reflect.
2. Another interesting activity involves using a map of the world and pictures as a point of departure. On the map, find Bali, Hawaii, and other islands. Discuss the climate and the style of life: a dance known as the *hula*; a style of cooking and a feast known as the *luau*. Start thinking of the backdrops and scenery you can build—the vivid colors, the erupting volcanos, the clear ocean waters, the straw skirts and *leis* and the types of huts lived in. Finally, begin the careful planning, drawing and building. Even if none of the numbers are staged, a great sense of accomplishment can be had by building the backdrops and some scenery with the recording played in the background.
3. Younger children will get great delight in dancing the *hula* (discussed more in the chapter on Fun Dances). Older pupils can delve more deeply into the entire culture and history of Hawaii. Even the

terrain and erupting volcanos can be explored. Do your pupils know that volcanos are a sure sign of life; that without volcanos, planets (including the earth) would be dead and cold, without the necessary heat to sustain life? Another angle to be explored is the historical perspective, going perhaps from the explorations of Captain Cook, to the continent of Australia, to the island of Hawaii becoming one of the United States. You might even go up to World War II, the attack on Pearl Harbor, the conflict with Japan, and the post-war period in Japan under General Douglas MacArthur.

4. Many music teachers have found that children enjoy the song "Dites-moi" because it is sung by children.

> *Dites-moi, pourquoi, la vie est belle*
> *Dites-moi, pourquoi, la vie est gai*
> *Dites-moi, pourquoi, chère mademoiselle*
> *Est-ce-que, parce que, vous m'aimez?*

THE KING AND I

Grades: K - 8

Materials: A recording of *The King and I*; pictures of Siam or Thailand including Siamese dress and temples; map of Asia.

Concepts:

1. The polka is a dance in 2/4 time.
2. Present day Thailand was once called Siam.

Activities
    &
Directions

1. From the novel *Anna and the King of Siam* came the successful Broadway adaptation, *The King and I*. Can your students find Siam or Thailand on the map? You might want to give them hints such as, "it is near China," or "it is close to Cambodia and Vietnam." Explain, that this is a part of the world known as southeastern Asia, and it used to be part of the French controlled Indo-China. Students interested in geography can learn that Bangkok is its capital, largest city, and chief seaport. Additional geographical facts are that the Gulf of Siam lies to the south, and to the west lies the arm of the Indian Ocean known as the Bay of Bengal. Mountain systems are the predominant feature of the terrain, although there is much fertile land. Monsoons and the frequent, seemingly incessant, rains of a

tropical climate characterize and shape its living style. With these facts as a backdrop, you might assign readings from the novel *Anna and the King of Siam*, or discuss the often touching story of Anna's trials and tribulations in being a teacher to the children of a petulant, impatient, and sometimes childish King. The end of the story is a tear-jerker, of course—so be prepared for sensitive pupils to cry.

2. We call this a "back to basics" lesson because, among the many exciting musical numbers in this show is a good old, ordinary, polka entitled "Shall We Dance," done by Anna and the King just before he gets very ill. Young children love its down-to-earth "two-beat rhythm." The easiest exercise in preparation for the number is to count ONE two, ONE two, ONE two, and so on. (Children can clap on ONE, or stomp on ONE, or do anything with a hard ONE on the downbeat. It can either be CLAP stomp, CLAP stomp, or STOMP clap, STOMP clap. One way is as good as another as long as the pupils *feel* the strong two-beat rhythm.) Another favored activity is to do the polka itself! Why not teach it to your students. Those who have seen the show know that it is an unforgettable scene, when the headstrong Anna tries to teach the even more headstrong King how to do the polka.

3. Two other favorites with very young children, are the "March of the Siamese Children," and "I Whistle a Happy Tune." Many music teachers have enjoyed using these numbers in their classroom teaching. Among the reasons for their success is that there are, indeed, so many children in the play—most of them, of course, being the King's own children. The march is another "basic" in music, being either a simple ONE two, ONE two, also, or a simple ONE two three four, ONE two three four. The whistling is something that music teachers have used successfully, in their teaching, for many years. Can your students whistle? Young children find it particularly difficult. If you teach them to whistle, you will be their friend for life! By the way, we have found that many pupils ask about Siamese cats and Siamese twins when we start on this play. You can tell them that the expression "Siamese twins" was coined when two children, in Siam, were born with their bodies united (in 1911).

4. Older pupils are also fascinated by the topic of Buddhism (the religion of most of the Thais). They can form study groups to compare it with Christianity. They can bring Buddhas (statues of Buddha) to school if friends and relations have any. This can be a starting point for discussing the conflict between Anna and the King. Which of his customs did she consider most immoral, for example? And in his song, "Is a Puzzlement," which of her traditions were

most puzzling? Some 7th and 8th grade students can report on the "basics" of Christianity and others can report on the "basics" of Buddhism.

Lest this entire chapter seem like a tribute to Richard Rodgers and Oscar Hammerstein, let us get on to some famous—but possibly less familiar—classics. We are going to touch upon such literary and operatic masterpieces as: *A Midsummer Night's Dream, Rosamunde, Rigoletto, Aida, La Bohème, Madame Butterfly, Carmen, The Flying Dutchman, Amahl and the Night Visitors*, and *The Medium*; we can then return to some equally profound, but in many ways lighter material, such as *Guys and Dolls, My Fair Lady,* and *West Side Story.* The idea is to use material of quality and substance and look for the fun-filled moments that young people can find in it. Again, find your own points of departure, your own embellishments, your own ways of adding the comic to the serious. Here's how some dramatists did it.

A MIDSUMMER NIGHT'S DREAM

Grades: 2 - 8

Materials: Shakespeare's original play *A Midsummer Night's Dream*; Mendelssohn's Overture and Incidental Music to Shakespeare's play *A Midsummer Night's Dream*; puppets or marionettes of fairies; wedding pictures of yourself and/or pupils' parents; wedding gowns that can be obtained from attics etc.; top hats or tuxedos.

Concepts:

1. A march is in 2/4 or 4/4 time (meter).
2. A prodigy is a very talented child.

**Activities
&
Directions**

1. Many consider Shakespeare the greatest dramatist in the history of mankind. Thus, Felix Mendelssohn's Overture and Incidental Music to *A Midsummer Night's Dream* represents another landmark of "wedding" drama and music. Pardon the pun, as we know that one of the more famous portions of the score is the popular "Wedding March." Did you know that Mendelssohn, a prodigy second only perhaps to Mozart, wrote the Overture when he was only seventeen years old? You might also share with your students the information that in 1843, King Frederick William IV of Prussia

requested Mendelssohn to write incidental music to several plays, *A Midsummer Night's Dream* being one. Related mathematical or map activities can be finding Prussia on a map of Europe, or computing the number of years this was before the start of the Civil War in the United States (Answer: 18) or the unification of Italy (Answer: 5) Another activity might be singing "Happy Birthday Dear Frederick" because the incidental music was first performed on October 14, 1843, on the eve of the festival of the King's birthday.

2. Younger children often have fun with the "Wedding Scene" and "Wedding March" which come after the close of Act IV. Some students can march down the aisle in full wedding dress (cut down or taken in of course), while others keep the beat of a march: ONE two three four, ONE two three four, ONE two three four, ONE two three four, etc. Many music teachers have had fun-filled lessons by bringing in their own wedding pictures so that their students can see what they looked like when they were younger (and thinner!). Another popular number is the "Fairy March" which comes in Act II. The "Fairy March" can be staged, (1) in costume, (2) with puppets, (3) with marionettes. By the way, can you yourself differentiate between the "Wedding March" from *Lohengrin* by Richard Wagner (more popularly known as "Here comes the Bride") and the Mendelssohn wedding march, which is most often played for the groom—or as an exit march after the marriage ceremony?

3. Older pupils can read the original play in its entirety. Whom will they find funniest: Snug, Bottom, Flute, Snout, Starveling, or Puck? Or will they find the fairies funniest: Cobweb, Moth, and Mustard-Seed? Puck is the jester, with most of the funniest lines; but Bottom, and Snout, and the Fairies do some funny things! Older students can also investigate the life and times of "the immortal bard," William Shakespeare (1564-1616), and the bearing this had on the play. For example, in a passage which describes Oberon's vision, a magnificent compliment is given to Queen Elizabeth I—she is referred to as "the imperial votaress." Oh well, let's get out our dictionaries! At any rate, the time in which Shakespeare lived (reflecting Queen Elizabeth), was known as the Elizabethan era; and the England of Shakespeare's day was known as Elizabethan England. On a map of England, you might find his birthplace, Stratford-on-Avon, and trace the Avon River. (We have mentioned the Shakespeare Memorial Theatre in his birthplace; and we have also discussed the Shakespeare festival held in this country, in Stratford *in Connecticut*, the city being named after the original. An excellent activity is to take

your pupils to a Shakespeare Festival that is close to your school and see this or another play.

ROSAMUNDE

Grades: 4 - 8

Materials: A recording of Schubert's incidental music to Rosamunde; map of Europe; pictures of a grand piano; pictures of the harp.

Concepts:

1. Schubert was one of the tragic figures in music, dying at the age of 31 in 1828.
2. Music known as "piano four hands" is for two pianists.

Activities
&
Directions

1. Many music teachers are fond of telling the story about Beethoven's and Schubert's graves being side by side in Vienna, Austria. Franz Schubert died tragically in 1828, as a young man, only one year after Beethoven's death. Beethoven was fifty-seven and Schubert was thirty-one—an interesting comparison. In only thirty-one years, Schubert was incredibly prolific (writing seven operas, six operettas, eight symphonies, eight overtures, fifteen string quartets, trios, quintets, octets, miscellaneous chamber music, and hundreds of songs!). As a background activity, you might have your pupils find Vienna, Austria, on a map of Europe, or, they might look at pictures of the grand piano and the harp (the overture to *Rosamunde* was originally composed for The Magic Harp, and later arranged for "piano four hands"). You might also explain that the nineteenth century was known as the "Romantic Era" because of the emotionality and the frequent "wedding" of the arts. Schubert, one of the greatest "romantics," spent many of his relaxing hours in coffee houses discussing literature and the theatre as well as music.

2. Another activity is to watch a television program with the sound off. This "homework activity" allows the children to try and envision what type of music should be used and see how it adds to the drama. In this way, a better perspective is gotten of the nineteenth century use of background or incidental music, as opposed to our own.

3. Some students find the full title of *Rosamunde* funny:

    Rosamunde, Fursten Von Cypern
    (Rosamunde, Princess of Cyprus)

If your pupils find the title funny, it is all right to capitalize on what has been called the "lightness of approach." If music is to be treated as fun, we must approach the serious from its lighter side. But be sure to use this silliness as a bridge to understanding and appreciation.

OPERA MINIATURES

Indeed, it is difficult to see the lighter side of some of the most famous serious operas. It may seem hard to have fun with a gruesome plot in which both the hero and the heroine get buried alive (*Aida*); where a father's plot backfires so that he opens up a sack and finds his dying daughter (*Rigoletto*); where the heroine is painfully dying of tuberculosis (*La Bohème*); where the heroine commits suicide (*Madama Butterfly*); or in which the jealous lover kills both the heroine and himself (*Carmen*). Yet, for generations, pupils introduced to these stories have found them comical rather than tragic—sort of like the unkind chuckle when watching someone slip on a banana peel. (All we are saying is that these emotions should be harnessed, rather than repressed or punished. The approach is different. If you expect and anticipate your students' laughing, you can share their reactions.)

After the full lesson on *Aida*, see if you can expand some of these ideas into a unit of study on understanding grand opera.

We define an opera miniature as a reenactment of one of an opera's most important or memorable scenes.

AIDA

Grades: K - 8

Materials: A recording of *Aida* by Guiseppe Verdi; toy or model pyramids; pictures of African headdresses and pictures of Egypt; map of Africa.

Concept:

Opera is a sung play, grand opera often being sung throughout, without any spoken dialogue. Grand opera may also contain spectacle in the form of ballet and/or elaborate dress and dance.

Activities
&
Directions

1. *Aida* was commissioned by the Egyptian Khedive to celebrate the inauguration of the Suez Canal. The Suez Canal was opened in November, 1869, but *Aida* was not produced until December 24, 1871 because of delays due to the Franco-Prussian War. Verdi refused the

commission at least twice. And, as with many of his operas, although he did not write the libretto, he and his wife modified it so much that for all intents and purposes both the music and the major features of plot were his. There are so many spectacular scenes that the work is a grand opera in the true Parisian sense of pomp and splendor, lavish scenery and costumes, and either ballet or grand dances. No greater wedding of drama and music exists than in grand opera, where music is meant to enhance the action and dramatic action inspires the creation of the music! Those who produce it have fun in doing so. If you can invite an opera producer to speak to your class, you will see the type of enthusiasm they have and generate! Just look through the entertainment (cultural events) section of your local newspaper, and you will see that there is an ever increasing number of small, local, opera companies.

2. The "opera miniature" that we love is the final scene in which Radames (an Egyptian warrior) is condemned to be buried alive with Aida (an Ethiopian slave who is really the daughter of the King of Ethiopia). This is a scene that pupils find fun to do against a backdrop of toy or specially built pyramids. Never mind the terrible fate of asphyxiation! The more the children say, "euhh, how horrible," the more they love it! It soon becomes easy to sneak in the rest of the plot: Princess Amneris's jealousy of Radames' love for Aida; Radames' victory over the Ethiopians; Aida's conflict between her love for Radames and her loyalty to her father and her country; and Aida's duplicity in obtaining military information for her father from Radames.

MORE OPERA MINIATURES

Since our Aida miniature wasn't all that miniature, here are some briefer plans for other opera miniatures.

Grades: 3 - 8

Materials: Recordings of and filmstrips for the following familiar operas: *Rigoletto, La Bohème, Madama Butterfly, Carmen, The Flying Dutchman, Amahl and the Night Visitors, The Medium*; a sleeping bag; rubber knives; a cot; café tables and candles; Japanese fans; a Japanese screen; recording of "The Star-Spangled Banner"; playing cards; a toy sword; an imitation bullfighter's cape; gypsy skirts or long colorful skirts; soldiers' and sailors' uniforms; a bullfighter's hat; pictures of storms and the sea.

Concepts:

1. We can have fun with opera (seeing it as sometimes overly serious, or perceiving some of the plots as bordering on the absurd).
2. We can teach a love and appreciation of opera as one of our greatest cultural heritages.

RIGOLETTO

Just as an explanation of the crypt scene in *Aida* brings reactions of "euhh" and "yuch," so too will your pupils make exclamations when they hear about Rigoletto carrying his dying daughter (Gilda) in a sack and about to cast her body into the river! (The deformed jester, Rigoletto, hired an assassin to kill the cursed Duke who had seduced his daughter; but instead, the assassin killed Rigoletto's daughter Gilda, who had changed places with the Duke whom she loved.) We have found that the scene pupils most love to reenact is Gilda coming out of the bag singing—a typical absurdity of opera that is frequently found to be comical. Another scene your pupils might love is the one in which the assassin Sparafucile (pronounced: Spara-foo-cheelay) kills Gilda instead of the Duke. We have also found that some children love to play the hunchbacked Rigoletto. And, since the text was adapted from a novel by Victor Hugo (*Le Roi S'Amuse*), you might want to mention *The Hunchback of Notre Dame* or any other famous hunchbacks in literature.

LA BOHÈME

Similar to Verdi's dying Guilda, still singing after she was placed in a sack and stabbed, is Giacomo Puccini's dying Mimi, still singing on her deathbed. Yet, in *La Bohème*, what might be considered a romantic tragedy, there is more than one scene of comic relief.

Many pupils like to play the opening scene of *La Bohème*, in which the almost penniless Bohemians get the landlord drunk to avoid paying the rent. You might have students improvise some dialogue while the recording is played very softly in the background.

Another light-hearted scene is one in which Musetta tricks her rich admirer Alcindoro. She gets him to pay the entire bill for a café party in the "Latin Quarter" of Paris (although he doesn't know about it because he is at the shoemaker's shop with a shoe that Musetta has pretended is too tight). A perfect musical background is the famous "Musetta's Waltz." You can create a Parisian cafe with candlelit tables and wine bottles.

Adults do not find it comical that poor Mimi is still singing as she is dying of tuberculosis, but some children do. We don't have to repress the giggles or titters; we can utilize the reaction. Some reaction is better than no reaction—and a reaction means responsiveness in some measure. Children love to imitate the dying Mimi (singing and falling, and then singing from what will be her deathbed). They will laugh at first, and then begin to see how sad it is. It will be good-natured fun that will culminate in appreciation and understanding through action. Props needed can be several chairs and/or a cot borrowed from the school nurse or Physical Education Department.

MADAMA BUTTERFLY

Another popular Puccini opera is *Madama Butterfly*. It depicts the tragic fate of a jilted heroine, Butterfly, who had been warned by a religious fanatic not to marry the American Lieutenant Pinkerton and abandon her faith. Some children may find humor in names such as "Cio-Cio-San" (Butterfly) and the U.S. consul "Sharpless." Even the names "Butterfly" and "Pinkerton" are funny to many children. Again, we suggest that the humor be harnessed and molded into insight and understanding.

After Pinkerton returns to Japan with his American wife, Butterfly knows that her marriage to Pinkerton had been duplicitous and false. She had renounced the faith of her ancestors and borne a child, only to be made a mockery of. When Pinkerton comes to take the child back to America with him, Butterfly appears to take it calmly but then commits suicide—a Japanese way of avoiding shame and "finding peace." How can this be humorous? Well, it's not really. But you have to know that in children's play, the act of *hari-kiri* (mispronounced harry-carry) is as commonplace as "Cowboys and Indians." They have fun in doing it, and it is a child's way of dealing with reality as well as with historical facts. The props might include a mat and a rubber knife. After all, walking the gangplank wasn't really fun to the sailors who went to their death this way. But in child's play it is another ritual used in fun. Try it and see if we are not right. Add a few fans and a Japanese screen and the set can be complete.

Madama Butterfly is one of several classical works that use a fragment of The *Star-Spangled Banner*. Listen to the opera beforehand so you can find out where it occurs. Then ask your class if they can hear where it is used. This is another activity you can use, and it might just be enough to help make your class sit through the entire work.

CARMEN

All children love to play a bullfighter (toreador) at some point during their childhood. They also love to play soldier. Bizet's opera *Carmen* gives them the opportunity to do both. There are also smugglers and gypsies—a complete cast of colorful characters for a child with a vivid imagination. Several of the girls, in Spanish costume, can have a street fight as in the first act of *Carmen*. Both boys and girls can try doing a gypsy dance as in the second act. At another point in the opera, Carmen and the gypsies use cards to tell her fortune (which is tragic); children love a scene that uses cards. At the end of the opera. Don José kills Carmen and then himself because she has rejected him in favor of the very exciting bullfighter Escamillo. Rubber knives will do nicely for props. Play the "Toreador Song" in the background.

THE FLYING DUTCHMAN

Playing a sailor should also be added to the list of "essentials" in children's play. The sea and ships are a part of every child's fantasy and imagination. Add a legend, a ghostly vessel, fate, and treasure, and you have an unbeatable combination. Richard Wagner must have thought so because, as with all of his operas, he wrote the text as well as the music. This fact makes Richard Wagner second to none as one of the all-around great creative geniuses. He was an innovator on many levels, even changing the harmonic vocabulary of western music. Wagner was truly one of the towering figures in the history of music.

Children can have fun using toy boats, or building large ones with wood, or painting them on canvas as a backdrop. The opening storm in the first act is fun to do. Your pupils will love flopping all over the place as the ship is buffeted by the storm. The exciting music would best be played on a cassette tape. Dialogue can be improvised around the legend of the Dutchman who is doomed to roam the sea eternally—coming ashore every seven years but not staying unless he can find a wife who will be true to him forever. We have found that doing this scene is enough to arouse curiosity about the rest of the opera (enabling us then to get into the characters of the Norwegian Sea Captain Daland and his daughter Senta).

AMAHL AND THE NIGHT VISITORS

Menotti's opera *Amahl and the Night Visitors* is a delightful Christmas presentation about an invalid boy who is visited by the three kings on their way to see the Christ child. We have found that children have tremendous sympathy for another child who has an infirmity; yet there are times when they can be cruel and must be helped in their development of understanding for afflictions. (This occasional cruelty can appear when they make fun of a child with a limp.) The set can be a house of a poor family with an invalid son; and the first task can be for several of your students to portray a youth who is completely or partially paralyzed. We can expect some initial laughter. But the fun can be channeled into joy of accomplishment as your class acts out the three kings paying a visit to the house. Another good role is the mother who at first thinks the poor boy is lying about the three kings. A song sung frequently is "Do you hear what I hear?"

THE MEDIUM

Another Gian-Carlo Menotti opera with characters of a mother and an infirm son is *The Medium*. In this opera, the mother is a medium who tricks clients into thinking that they have contacted relatives who are deceased. The tragedy of this opera is that, after pangs of conscience and deciding to "go straight," the mother accidentally murders her own son!

We have had great success in staging part of this opera as an opera miniature. You will find that your pupils love to have a séance. The lights go out; candles are lit perhaps; a table is made to rise in some way; there are weird noises made and some students "throw" their voices to imitate clients being duped into thinking that they hear the voice of a son or husband who has been killed. The basic subject matter is sad and tragic. But the activity is great fun to many, many children. Being in the dark is "spooky" and fun, like Halloween. Using a bedsheet to hide behind and from which to make "sounds from the beyond" is a fun-filled activity. And even the tragedy of a mother shooting her son accidentally is one of those "eeow how horrible" types of fun. The music is palatable enough, and just spooky enough to be played softly in the background as the stage business and improvised dialogue takes place.

BACK TO BROADWAY MINIATURES

Grades: 3 - 8

Materials: Recordings and/or scores of *My Fair Lady, West Side Story*, and *Guys and Dolls.*

Concepts:

1. *Opera* means work: *opera musica* means musical work.
2. Our American Broadway musical comedy is the equivalent of the German *singspiel*, the French *opera comique*, and the Italian *opera buffa*.

Returning now to Broadway, we can take great comfort in the fact that no less a genius than Kurt Weill felt that Broadway would be the avenue down which American opera would travel. After all, in its broadest (or strictest) sense, *opera* means "work," and the term *opera* is actually a shortening of "Opera in Musica," meaning musical work. Opera, then, can be defined as a sung play—many of the operas we know have spoken dialogue.

Not until the nineteenth century in general, and Richard Wagner in particular, were most of the operas sung completely throughout. The eighteenth century had *singspiel* in Germany, *opera comique* in France, and *Opera Buffa* in Italy (all of which were the equivalent of our musical comedy, and all of which had spoken dialogue).

MY FAIR LADY

George Bernard Shaw was one of the great wits in English playwriting history. His *Pygmalion* was based upon the Greek legend of the statue that was molded to perfection and came to life. When Lerner and Loewe collaborated to set this play to music, it became another great marriage of drama and music. The humor of "Why Can't a Woman Be More Like a Man" might be a bit above first through fourth graders. But fifth graders and older students can begin to relate to it. In fact, the "girl-hating" third and fourth graders might relate well to it, indeed. The "facts" can be changed to fit the age.

Two other songs from *My Fair Lady* that we have had success with are, "The Rain in Spain," and "I Could Have Danced All Night." Henry Higgins taught Liza Doolittle that "The rain in Spain stays mainly on the plain," to help her overcome her cockney accent. See if your pupils get tongue-tied, or have fun rolling the "r" in rrrain! Young girls sometimes have fun with "I Could Have Danced All Night" by dancing around with a doll.

WEST SIDE STORY

One of several links between Shakespeare and the American Broadway comedy or music drama is *West Side Story* (another, for example, is *Kiss Me Kate*, made into a musical from Shakespeare's *The Taming of the Shrew*). Students from kindergarten through high school get energized by the thought of the Jets versus the Sharks, or of both gangs making fun of Officer Krupke. Other well known songs are, "Tonight," "Maria," "America," and "Somewhere." The street scenes that you can stage are: (1) set up the rumble (gang fight) between the Jets and the Sharks, and try to emphasize the Italian versus Puerto Rican differences (easier said than done without getting into insulting stereotypes); (2) set up the scene in which everyone makes fun of Officer Krupke, with or without some type of a policeman's uniform (sometimes a friendly policeman will good-naturedly come in to school to play the part); (3) set up the scene in which there is the inevitable dance in the school gym; (4) stage a modernized version of the famous balcony scene in which Juliet originally said to Romeo, "Romeo, Romeo, wherefore art thou Romeo?" and (5) stage the popular "I want to be in America" scene with colorful flared skirts—for Puerto Rican Discovery Day perhaps.

All of the above can be done better, of course, with several hearings of the recorded music. We have found that the original Shakespeare story, and the updated *West Side Story*, both are so popular and idea-inspiring that many pupils will surprise you with the ideas they'll come up with!

GUYS AND DOLLS

Our final selection, although this list of opera and Broadway favorites is by no means complete, is the collage of Damon Runyon characters in the funny musical entitled *Guys and Dolls*. With white suits, black shirts, white ties, and "tough guy" hats, our favorite scene is the one in which the boys and girls dress up like gamblers and gun molls. We've had great success with this activity. Use simple props such as a news stand and racing forms. Play the "Fugue for Tinhorns" from *Guys and Dolls*, which starts off with "I got the horse right here, his name is Paul Revere. . ." Children love this skit and you should also! It is great fun!

If you are into celebrating musical birthdays, you might want to place on the chalkboard:

OPENING OF GUYS AND DOLLS
(November 24, 1950)

Compute how many years ago this was, if you want a related mathematics activity; and then go on to reading some of Damon Runyon's short stories for a related reading activity.

5

Fun
Dances

Perhaps there is nothing more enjoyable in music than dancing. Dancing is pure fun; and one has only to watch youngsters at a party or clustered around a jukebox to come to this realization. Why not use all of this energy as a stepping stone, as a point of departure for not only having fun but also for learning musical concepts? Polkas are in 2/4 or 4/4 time with two or four beats to the measure—this is sometimes called *duple meter*. Waltzes are in 3/4 time with three beats to the measure, sometimes called *triple meter*. These and other concepts can be dealt with in a fun-filled atmosphere, abounding with all types of energetic rhythms! Teachers have little difficulty getting students to do the "Mexican Hat Dance" or the "Alley Cat." We hope you will have as much fun with this chapter as we did in preparing it for you. Have fun!

Figure 8

FAT DOT FUN

Grades: 3 - 8

Materials: Chalk and chalkboard or music flash cards.

Concepts:

1. Each letter of the alphabet can open up a world of music.
2. The music staff, the bass or F clef, and eighth notes.

**Activities
&
Directions**

1. Place Figure 8 on the chalkboard or on music flash cards. Explain that the first symbol they see is an F or bass clef. Have them practice drawing it several times. We have called it the "funny" clef or the "fat-dot" clef to help the pupils remember that it designates "F." [You might want to start with a single line, making a fat dot on it. Now if this is to be the fourth line (Fat dot on the Fourth line), we must draw a line above it and three lines below it, since we know that a staff has five lines.] We have used Figure 9 to demonstrate what eighth notes look like.

Figure 9

2. "I thought this was a chapter on dancing," you might be saying! Well, why not name some dances beginning with "F" for the fat-dot or funny clef. We can only think of the fox trot or the "F" in folk dances for now. How many can you and your students name? How about using the "A" in Figure 8. (Answer: Alley Cat). Next use the "C" in Figure 8 and name the cancan, for example. Our last eighth note in Figure 8 is "E", and we can't think of any dances. Can you? Finally, if you can make a large enough poster or floor diagram of Figure 8, your pupils can create a dance step based on the pattern of the eighth notes on the staff. Try it; it's fun.

3. Using the eighth note "C" in Figure 8, you can also bridge the gap between fun dances in the pop and folk field, and have fun with music of a more serious nature. For the letter "C," we can name Chopin, a ballet choreographed by Jerome Robbins called *The Concert* (Concert), choreography, and charade. The charades that are in the ballet *The Concert* are among the funniest in the ballet repertory—and we wish everyone could see it. (It is about an onstage concert of Chopin music, in which the dancers portray the people who are attending the concert. All the annoyances of a concert are satirized, as people bother other people who are trying to listen to the music. Using a few simple props, your pupils can stage some similar antics. For example, it is easy to stage the annoying experience of one person with a large hat sitting right in front of someone who is just getting completely absorbed in the music of Chopin (or something equally as beautiful). Simple charades that are funny will give us the feeling of the humor in this ballet.

SPINNING AND JUMPING ROPE

Grades: K - 4

Materials: Jump rope; motion picture camera; camera; photographs of sports figures in action.

Concept:

Many of a young child's movements are dance-like.

Activities
&
Directions

How many of the young child's movements are almost dances in themselves—physical poses that, if videotaped or filmed, would stand up as a type of dance? Think of some groups of children jumping rope, for example. The movements are very dance-like. Use them as an introduction to the concept of fun dances. Not all dances have to be to music. The movements of a bee, to tell other members of the nest and hive where the pollen is, is called a dance. The strutting of a peacock is a type of a dance. Thus, among the energizers you can use are many of the games that children play. Think of the many variations on "Engine, Engine Number 9" that seem to exist all over these United States. We bet that at least one of your students has at some time recited, ". . . if the train goes off the track, will you get your money back?"

For these and other reasons, we believe that the type of "spinning" done by many children is a type of a dance. In the next lesson on carrousels, we refer to this spinning in the "Activities and Directions" section. Add your own activities of course, which can be jokes, riddles, games, limericks, cartoons, puzzles, or stories. Look for poses and stances that are dance-like and can be used to create new dances (someone had to create the dances we do; why not us for a change?). Be sure to include action photos of sports heros!

CARROUSELS

Grades: K - 8

Materials: Pictures of carrousels and merry-go-rounds; miniature or toy carrousels and merry-go-rounds; jewelry boxes that play carrousel or merry-go-round music.

Concepts:

1. Much of the music used for carrousels and merry-go-rounds is in 3/4 or "waltz time." Waltz time is the grouping of beats in threes with a heavy emphasis on the first beat.
2. Carrousels and merry-go-rounds combine large-scale sweeping movements with music.

Activities
&
Directions

1. Young children love to spin—with or without music. Have you ever watched children spin until they get dizzy, and then start going the other way? Why not have them spin with music? We have found that they seem to have almost as much fun as when they initiate the activity themselves. Music boxes can be used, or recorded music of piano rolls that are used for the carrousel.
2. Older children may be more aware of Rodgers and Hammerstein's Broadway musical, *Carousel*. If not, you can introduce the many beautiful melodies in the score such as the *Carousel* theme itself, which is a famous waltz. While playing this theme, older children can think both ONE, two, three, ONE, two, three, and OOM, pah, pah, OOM, pah, pah. You can explain that this is the meaning of waltz or three quarter time (the grouping of beats by threes). Younger children can have fun by making believe they are on a carrousel. Older students can also investigate whether carrousels and merry-go-rounds are the same or not. They can also look for songs which contain references to carrousels or merry-go-rounds.

NAME THAT DANCE

Grades: 3 - 8

Materials: Pictures of dancers doing the tango, Charleston, waltz or square dances.

Concept:

The names of dances stimulate visual associations.

Activities
&
Directions

1. Ask your students to name dances or dance steps they know. To ones they name, you might add:

Bunny Hop	Lindy
Hokey Pokey	Conga
Alley Cat	Samba
Charleston	Monkey
Rhumba	Hula
Tango	Square Dance
Twist	Virginia Reel
Mambo	Waltz
Cha Cha	Polonaise
Merengue	Minuet

Another interesting activity is to elicit "associations" to the dances you name. Will *tango* conjure up a vision of Rudolph Valentino, or a robust Argentine *gaucho* with his female companion in her wide skirt? Will the *Charleston* conjure up visions of the flappers? Have any of your students seen anyone do the *peabody*, the *pasa doble*, or the *hully gully*? What are their impressions?

2. Some students like to ask you about dances they've seen in a movie or cartoon, but don't know the names of. This is an interesting activity, as the pupils try to describe the movements they've seen and hope you know what they mean.

THE CANCAN

Grades: K - 8

Materials: Pictures of France and French saloons; pictures of dancers doing the cancan; slides of Paris that include the Eiffel Tower and other famous sights; skirts with ruffles and crinolines; a recording of

Gaité Parisienne by Jacques Offenbach that includes the famous cancan.

Concepts:

1. The unique rhythmic movement in the cancan is the way the legs are kicked out on the "off beats" of TWO and FOUR.
2. Some dances can represent, and make us immediately think of, a country—the cancan is one.

Activities
&
Directions

1. We have found this one of the easiest dances with which to start—one of the reasons being that the boys can dance with the boys, and the girls with the girls; they don't have to touch each other! When children are at the "boys hating girls" and "girls hating boys" stages, one cannot get them to dance with the opposite sex. This dance permits some healthy competition between the two groups. Of course, the dance was originally done by women; but the boys can be motivated to try to outdo the girls by phrases such as, "Men, can you kick your legs higher than the girls can?" or using tongue-twisters such as, "Boys, can do the cancan better than the girls can do the cancan?" (How about: if the boys can't do the cancan better than the girls can do the cancan, who can do the cancan better than I can do the cancan?)
2. Related activities can include:
   a. looking at pictures and slides of Paris or other parts of France;
   b. finding Paris on a map of France and/or finding France on a map of Europe;
   c. taking a trip to a French restaurant;
   d. playing French games;
   e. listening to *Gaité Parisienne* by Jacques Offenbach that includes his famous cancan. Explain that this is the most famous music for the dance but that it was not the only piece of music to which the cancan was danced;
   f. bringing some costumes to school or sewing skirts especially for the occasion.

A WEDDING, BAR MITZVAH
OR CHRISTENING

Dancing is among the more enjoyable experiences people have with music. People seem to have the most fun when dancing at a wedding or other family occasion. Yet, the exuberance from this activity is rarely transferred to a school situation. Why not capitalize on the planned and spontaneous use of music as fun, in dancing? It is at a wedding that so many of the different fun dances are performed: the Alley Cat, bunny hop, Mexican Hat Dance, jig, tarantella, or hora—as well as the fox trot, waltz, cha cha, polka, merengue, and the very latest dances. At a wedding, we so often add pride in our roots to the pride we have as Americans; and, rather than detract, this pride adds zest (salt and pepper) to the evening's activities. As teachers, we should try to "bottle" some of this spirit and bring it into the classroom; we should nurture the zeal and add it to any enthusiasm that we already have developed, by accepting that which children feel is relevant (for example, the music of the peer group and of the media). In the lessons that follow, we wish to help you recall many of the dances that you may well have done at the last big wedding, family affair or party you attended. If you had fun doing the steps then, have fun with it again in the classroom and share this fun with your students!

THE MEXICAN HAT DANCE

Grades: K - 8

Materials: Recording of The Mexican Hat Dance; a large sombrero or a picture of one; optional materials are foods such as tortillas, enchiladas or tacos.

Concepts:

1. The Mexican Hat Dance is one of the best universally acclaimed fun dances.
2. It is one of the most frequently played dances at weddings and other celebrations because it so easily leads into other dances such as the tarantella, jig, hora, or the polka.
3. The Mexican Hat Dance is an excellent springboard—both to get everybody up and also to get the blood circulating.

Activities
&
Directions

The simple dance step involves simultaneously thrusting the left foot forward as the right one goes back, then alternating the procedure so that the right foot goes forward as the dancer leaps up and the left foot goes back! Easier done than said! Don't forget the hesitation after the third leap, which can be represented by a musical rest (in this case a quarter rest ♩).

You might try having a cabaret "set-up" in which one student imitates a frustrated Master of Ceremonies, desperately trying to get everyone up to dance. Suddenly, the Mexican Hat Dance is played and everyone gets into a big circle. The trick is doing eight sets of three leaps and then pause. After this set of eight, the dancers go into another dance where you normally have the couples joining elbows, swinging first to the right (clockwise), then to the left (counterclockwise). Several different dances are used alternately. In this cabaret set-up, part of the fun is to have spicy Mexican foods. (Make sure to include several pitchers of water.) Whether or not you can use candles is probably up to your building principal. Request permission before you do anything that can be dangerous.

For added fun, place a large hat in the center of the dancing area. Dancers leap over it or dance around it—but *never* do they step on it. Younger children can have added fun by dressing up in Mexican costumes.

THE HORA

Grades: 1 - 8

Materials: Recordings of Israeli horas that include the song "Hava Nagila" or "Come and Be Joyful" (Folkcraft 1110B, Folkcraft 1116A, RCA Victor LPM 1623, or Educational Dance Recordings FD-2); the chapter on "Easy Folk Dances for Elementary Grades" from Richard G. Kraus's book *Folk Dancing*, page 71.*

Concepts:

1. The hora is an Israeli dance of happiness.
2. *Hava Nagila* means "come let us rejoice."

**Activities
&
Directions**

1. The hora is a dance performed at many Jewish weddings to express joy and happiness. It is a circle dance in which the dancers join hands or arms, facing in. Any good book on ethnic dances should have a detailed explanation. The easiest to follow is the one mentioned above in Richard G. Kraus's *Folk Dancing*. It is done to the fairly well-known song, "Hava Nagila"; you and your class should have a great deal of fun. Your school's physical education teacher might also help you and your pupils learn how to do the dance correctly.

*Richard G. Kraus, *Folk Dancing: A Guide for Schools, Colleges and Recreation Groups,* © 1962 by Richard G. Kraus. Cited with permission of the Macmillan Co., New York.

The simplest way of doing the hora is as follows:

> *Step to the left with your left foot.*
> *Place your right foot behind the left.*
> *Step to the left again; then, hopping on the left foot,*
> *swing your right foot in front of it.*
> *Step on the right foot in place; then, hopping on it,*
> *swing the left foot in front of it.*

2. You might want to stage your own wedding scene. There was one staged in the Broadway production of *Fiddler on the Roof*, and it can be used as a model. Be sure to include.the hora as part of the activities.

THE TARANTELLA

Grades: 2 - 8

Materials: A recording of Italian Neapolitan songs and dances that include the dance, the tarantella; a recording of the *Grand Tarantella* for piano and orchestra by Gottschalk; rubber toy spiders; dress for a wedding; map of Italy.

Concepts:

1. One explanation of the derivation of the name *tarantella* is that it probably originated in Taranto, Apulia.
2. Another explanation of why the dance was named *tarantella* is that the bite of the large spider, Lycosa tarantula, was supposed to cause a frenzy of dancing.

Activities
&
Directions

1. A disease prevalent in Italy in the fifteenth, sixteenth, and seventeenth centuries, called tarantism, was commonly laid to the effects of a spider's bite, and was said to be curable only by dancing to the point of exhaustion. At the height of the epidemics, bands of musicians wandered through the countryside playing the various tunes which were supposed to provide a cure. You might use this information as a backdrop for the dance activities in this lesson. Younger students might even like the silliness of using one of those rubber spiders to "inspire" a frenzy of dancing in one another.
2. Just as the hora was used in a Jewish wedding scene in the last lesson, the tarantella can be used as part of an Italian wedding scene—or an Italian feast. An added attraction of such a lesson can be serving

Italian foods. Why not invest in an Italian cook book if you and your students get sufficiently inspired. Of course, for the wedding scene, you will also need some cut-down wedding dresses and tuxedos or black suits.

3. The easiest way to begin the tarantella is by arranging pupils in pairs or couples. First, place the hands on the waist and throw the head way back. As the music begins either "high step" or kick out with the heel first hitting the ground. Next, the couples spin around each other in a variety of ways: one way is back-to-back as in an American square dance; another is by joining arms at the elbows and going around to the right first and then to the left.

4. A related map activity is to find Naples, which Italians call Napoli. Can you find Taranto, Apulia, where the tarantella may have begun?

THE JIG

Grades: 2 - 8

Materials: A recording of Irish dances including the *jig*; map of Great Britain (including Ireland); pictures of bagpipes and kilts; Joan Lawson's book, *European Folk Dance* (New York: Pitman Publishing Co., 1972), p. 175.

Concepts:

1. The *jig* or *gigue* is a fast dance of supposed English origin, and is in 6/8 or triple time.
2. The *jig* is done on festive occasions.

Activities & Directions

1. Among the fun dances done at Irish-American weddings is the *jig*. As the hora and the tarantella were used in structured wedding scenes in this chapter, so too can the *jig* be used as part of an Irish-American wedding scene—or an Irish-American party. If you have any students who have an Irish kilt and/or Irish bagpipes, there can be added zest to this lesson. Otherwise, pictures of kilts and bagpipes can be used. Have your students ever seen the St. Patrick's Day parade televised? If they have, the visual image is set and the dance we describe can be in the mind's eye.
2. The lucky teacher will have a student who can demonstrate the Irish

jig. Descriptions of the jig vary greatly. You may find some descriptions in books on country dances, European folk dances, or dances of the British Isles. It might be best to get some assistance from your school's physical education teacher, or even try to bring in a local expert. Many square dance callers know how to explain the jig as it has many similarities to the reel.

At Irish American weddings, the "lilt" or Irish step dancing is often done. Descriptions of step dancing may be found in the same books as the jig. In doing the dance, an Irish "step-dancer" will keep his hands straight at his sides. As the strong beat of the music is felt (and people in a circle often clap their hands in time to the music), the step-dancer sort of hops on one foot while performing fancy leg-work with the other. This is really difficult to describe; it involves bending the leg at the knee as the leg is raised above the waist, and the toe is pointed first to the left and then to the right. The important thing is that a jig is played, a circle is formed, the pupils in the circle start clapping in time to the music, the step-dancer goes to the center of the circle, and the hopping and kicking motions begin.

3. To feel the 6/8 time of the jig, the pupils in the circle can clap ONE two three, FOUR five six, ONE two three FOUR five six. Figure 10 can be placed on the chalkboard to show that these six beats or pulses can be six eighth notes.

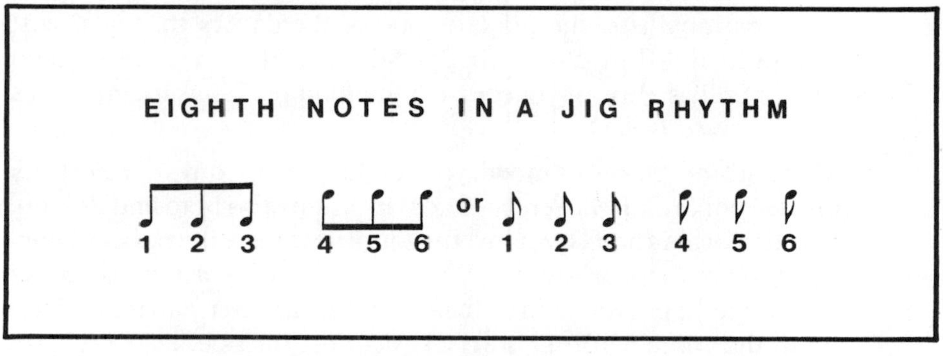

EIGHTH NOTES IN A JIG RHYTHM

1 2 3   4 5 6   or   1 2 3   4 5 6

Figure 10

THE POLKA

Grades: 2 - 8

Materials: Recordings of polkas; pictures of authentic Polish or German polka dancers with colorful costumes; picture of a tuba; map of Europe.

Concepts:

1. The sharp and the flat.
2. The tuba is used in many polka bands.
3. The polka is a sharply accented dance in 2/4 or 4/4 time that originated in Bohemia (now Czechoslovakia) and was called the *Pulka* in Czech.

Activities
   &
Directions

1. The polka is a dance that makes children smile when they see it done. Perhaps that is because people sometimes look funny as they hop about, first in one direction then in another (the same is true, of course, for some other dances also). At any rate, being primarily interested in making music fun, we certainly are glad when pupils see anything that makes them giggle a little. We hope that those beautiful smiles remain when you teach them the very simple basic two-step of the polka—and also remain when the students actually start doing it themselves! After all, think of the fun that people have when doing the polka at a wedding. This is most often true for Polish-American or German-American weddings, where the polka is one of the more frequently played dances. But even at weddings of other nationalities, the polka is one of the dances that is almost always included in the evening's festivities. (there are well-known Italian polkas also, and of course Bohemian polkas as in Smetana's *The Bartered Bride.*)

2. To create the setting, or mood, you might show pictures of colorfully dressed polka dancers. A related activity might also be to find Poland, Czechoslovakia and Germany, the countries where the polka is often done, on a map of Europe. Then you can have a type of polka party—perhaps even with authentic Polish and German foods. Decorate the room with all sorts of pictures. Include also, perhaps, pictures of tubas; and ask your students if they can hear the deep sound of the tuba on some recordings of polka music. Have any seen polka "Oom Pah" bands?

3. For upper grades there should be at least one lesson about fun dances that introduce some basic musical concepts. Well, here we are! Place Figure 11 on the chalkboard or on musical flash cards.

   In Figure 11A, we see first a half note "G"; then we see a dotted quarter note "G"; then we see an eighth note F sharp (note that the sharp($\sharp$) is placed before the note and not after it). Do you remember

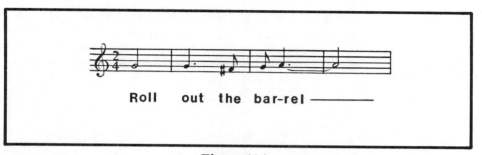

Figure 11A

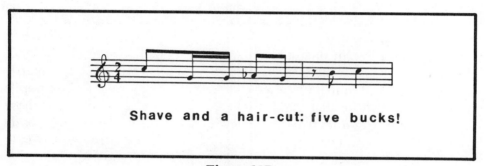

Figure 11B

why the notes are "G" and "F"? Do you remember E G B D F (*Every Good Boy Does Fine*, or, as in merry old England, *Every Good Boy Deserves Favour*)? Do you remember F A C E as the letter names of the four spaces? Thus, the first note is a "G" because it is on the second line (Every Good), and the third note is an "F" because it is in the first space (*F, A, C, E*). Therefore, what are the fourth and fifth notes? (Answer: the fourth is the same as the first two—"G"; the fifth is "A" because it is in the second space—as in F,A of F A C E.)

In Figure 11B, we see eighth notes, sixteenth notes, an eighth rest, a quarter note, and a flat sign. We know you and your pupils can figure out the "Shave and a haircut" rhythm. So now, look for the flat sign (♭). Look also for the eighth rest (𝄾). Now, find the sixteenth notes 𝅘𝅥𝅰𝅘𝅥𝅰 and differentiate them from the eighth notes 𝅘𝅥𝅮𝅘𝅥𝅮 . Which ones have two crossbars?

Did we forget to mention that Figure 11B is the way many polkas end? (At least, that is the way many experienced dance band musicians end a polka!) It may not be the original ending, but, when not sure how to stop, that's what they use. A fun activity is to dance the polka; then, when someone sings or claps the "Shave and a haircut" rhythm, the dancers have to stop.

Are you ready to review all the notes in figures 11A and 11B? See

Figure 12 and try matching notes and signs with the musical examples as they appeared on the five lines of the staff.

Symbol	Note Name	Measure
♩	_____	_____
♩.	_____	_____
♪	_____	_____
♫	_____	_____
♩♩	_____	_____
⸚	_____	_____
𝄾	_____	_____
𝄿	_____	_____
♯	_____	_____
♭	_____	_____

Figure 12

THE HOKEY POKEY

Grades: K - 8

Materials: A recording of the Hokey Pokey; music flashcards (optional).

Concepts:

1. Left hand and right hand; left foot and right foot.
2. The dotted eighth note and sixteenth note. ♪. ♬

Activities
&
Directions

1. You may think that all students are well coordinated, know the parts of the body, and can quickly use the left and right hands or specific fingers. Well, the truth of the matter is that many can't. Thus, for younger children you can have the satisfaction of being an important influence in making sure they learn their left and right hands, their left and right feet, and other parts of the body. With this dance—that we have seen bringing great joy to both children in classrooms and adults at weddings or parties—your students will be making important verbalizations while improving coordination. The words of the directions to the dance are (and dancers usually sing along):

> *You put your left hand in*
> *You put your left hand out*
> *You put your left hand in*
> *And you shake it all about*
> *You do the hokey pokey*
> *And you turn yourself around*
> *That's what it's all about.*

In this dance, the dancers are all in a circle. Everyone follows the leader's directions. When the leader says "left hand in," the dancers raise their left hands and point them toward the center of the circle; "left hand out" means raised hands pointing out and away from the center of the circle; "doing the Hokey Pokey" means hands raised slightly above the head with pointer and middle finger in the "V" for victory sign, bending from side to side with the shoulders being lowered and raised, and turning completely around until one is in the exact same position facing the center of the circle. This being completed, the dancers are now ready to follow directions such as:

> You put your right hand in
> (complete as with left hand)
>   etc.
> You put your left foot in
>   etc.
> You put your head in
>   etc.

Younger students can have even more fun and learn more parts of the body by using directions not normally used with adults: you put your pinky in; you put your ring finger in; you put your ankle in; etc.

2. For older students, the Hokey Pokey affords an excellent opportunity for teaching the rhythm of the dotted eighth followed by a sixteenth note (see Figure 13). Place Figure 13 on the chalkboard or on music flash cards.

Figure 13

You might want your pupils to copy the music notes so they can have the experience of drawing them. They can then clap the rhythm quite accurately by thinking of any word that has a long – short syllable combination. Drummers sometimes have their pupils think of the jazz use of the cymbal and have them say:

Figure 14

You will notice, in Figure 14, that right after the dotted eighth followed by a sixteenth note rhythm, there is a single quarter note. Now, how is this used in the dance? Quite simply. See Figure 15. Have observers clap the rhythm as the dancers perform the action.

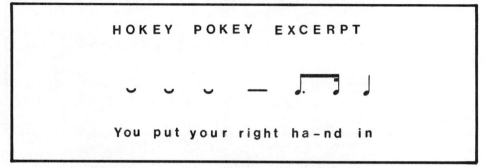

Figure 15

THE ALLEY CAT

Grades: K - 6

Materials: A recording of *The Alley Cat.*

Concepts:

　1. The quarter note and quarter rest.
　2. A note head is oval shaped.

**Activities
　&
Directions**

　　The Alley Cat is one of the most frequently asked for game dances at a wedding. How many of your pupils know it? For younger pupils, it is excellent for teaching "oneness" and "twoness" or the concepts of "once" and "twice." It also teaches coordination using the simple movements involved in clapping and jumping. It can also illustrate the concepts of a quarter note and a quarter rest.

　　The words of the directions are as follows:

> *Your right foot to the right (twice)*
> *And your left foot to the left (twice)*
> *Your right back twice*
> *And your left back twice*
> *Your right across twice (over the left knee)*
> *And your left across twice (over the right knee)*
> *Right (across the left knee once)*
> *Left (across the right knee once)*

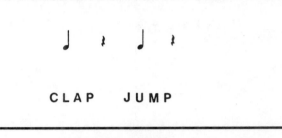

CLAP   JUMP

Figure 16

or

Right foot, right foot, left foot left
Right back right back, left back left
Right across, right across, left across left
Right across, left across, clap, jump.

You may notice that the clap and the jump can be represented by quarter notes and the beats in between them can be represented by quarter rests. Perhaps you might like to explain to your students that a quarter note receives one beat (in 4/4 time) and so does a quarter rest. They can practice drawing quarter notes, perhaps, by drawing an oval, adding the stem then filling in the oval. (See Figure 17.)

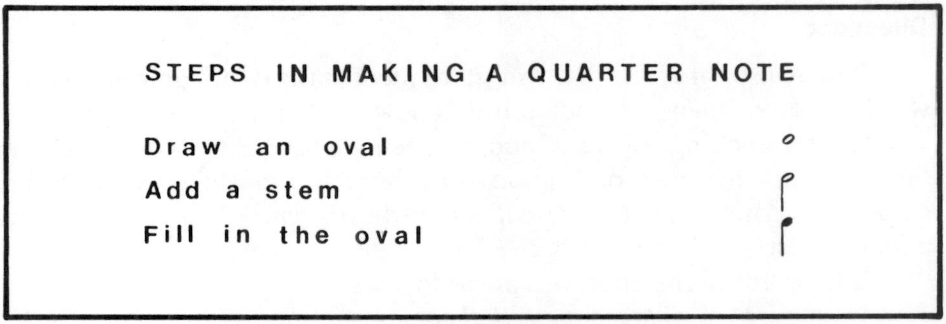

STEPS   IN   MAKING   A   QUARTER   NOTE

Draw   an   oval   o

Add   a   stem   ♩

Fill   in   the   oval   ♩

Figure 17

Many music teachers like to point out that the note head looks more like a football than a circle. What do you and your students think? And, what do they think of the quarter rest? ♩

6

Things Found Funny and Funny Sounds

Included in this chapter are sounds that will make children laugh or giggle—sometimes snicker. You can make some of these sounds yourself if you can obtain the right materials. Others can be found on recordings which we suggest. With a small investment of time, you and your students can get some good chuckles! Whether it be braying, buzzing, growling, crowing, fluttering, whistling, or fiddling, there will be something that is sure to cause a smile.

BRAYING, BUZZING, GROWLING AND CROWING

Grades: 3 – 7

Materials: Various brass instrument mouthpieces (trumpet, trombone, French horn, or tuba); oboe and/or bassoon reed; pictures of the trumpet, French horn, trombone, and tuba; recordings of the saxophone; pictures of crows, dogs, donkeys; map of Europe (especially Belgium and France).

Concepts:

1. To play high notes on brass instruments you must tighten the lips; one way to tighten up is to make a puckered smile.
2. The clarinet and saxophone both use a single reed; the oboe and the bassoon use a double reed.

Activities
&
Directions

1. We have found that the concept of the puckered smile is both "found funny" and produces laughter—especially when we explain: "first you smile then you pucker," or, "first you pucker then you smile!" Using mouthpieces for brass instruments, that you have obtained from a local music store or a music supply outlet, your objective is to teach the process of "buzzing," something that is done with all brass instrument mouthpieces. As we said, many pupils find this very funny—especially since you can slobber all over the place as you try to get your lips to vibrate, or buzz, properly. Can you vibrate your lips and get "Three Blind Mice" or "Row, Row, Row Your Boat"? If you are vibrating your lips properly, you should be able to play these and other songs using your lips alone. Here's where the puckered smile comes in: smile, then pucker, then vibrate; or, pucker, then smile, then vibrate. The next step is to do this into one or all of the brass mouthpieces. After you have perfected your technique, teach the procedure to your class and be ready for plenty of chuckles!

2. Now that you know the funniness of buzzing, you might try "braying." The fun can be enhanced, we have found, with a nice, large picture of a donkey. Actually, the sound we are thinking of is not made too often by brass players (particularly the trumpet). You can picture the sound by thinking of the opening fanfare before a horse race. Using the mouthpiece of your choice, start high and tight, then quickly loosen up while blowing. We have found that this produces a sound that sounds like braying, and results in a fun lesson. By the way, it is also an excellent way of starting third graders on blowing mouthpieces for brass instruments. Older students find it fun too!

3. Another enjoyable activity is "crowing" (the term used for the sound made when blowing into the double-reeds used for oboes and bassoons. Guaranteed, that just as your pupils will laugh when you first demonstrate buzzing, they will laugh when you demonstrate crowing. Of course, you can enhance the fun by hanging up some pictures of crows. Fun can also be had by trying to draw crows yourselves. With fifth through seventh graders, you might also want to get a little more serious and explore the backgrounds of these double-reed instruments. Explain that the oboe is one of the most ancient wind instruments of conical bore. The shawm or primitive oboe was found in Egyptian tombs of 3700 B.C. It was the composer Handel's favorite, and two oboes were used routinely in the eighteenth century orchestrations of Haydn and Beethoven.

4. "Growling" is a sound that can be made with the saxophone. Recordings made by players such as Eddie "Lockjaw" Davis, Eddie Harris, Coleman Hawkins, Phil Kensie or Boots Randolph, demonstrate what we mean. Many saxophone solos on rock 'n roll recordings of the 1950's also use this style of "growling." Both the term and the sound make many pupils laugh. Starting with this fun (adding the activity of drawing growling dogs perhaps) you can then get more serious. Explain that the saxophone was invented by Adolphe Sax. His father, Charles Joseph Sax (1791-1865), was even more important in the history of music. He was a Belgian-French instrument maker, born in Dinant-sur-Meuse. (Can you and your pupils find it on a map of Belgium?) In 1815 he established himself in Brussels (easier to find on a map) and soon became especially known for his brass instruments. After long investigation and experimentation, he discovered the exact proportion for the scale of wind instruments that was most conducive to a full round tone. Together with his son Adolphe, he made many improvements in musical instruments. Adolphe was born in 1814. (Do your students know about the War of 1812? What was Napoleon Bonaparte doing at this time?) Charles Joseph Sax died in 1865. Do your pupils know that this was the year that the Civil War ended? What was happening during the year of his birth (1791)? In Europe? In the United States? (By the way, Mozart died in 1791 at the young age of 35.)

BASSOONS AND CONTRABASS SARRUSOPHONES

Grades: 3 – 7

Materials: Pictures of a bassoon, a contrabassoon, a contrabass sarrusophone; recordings of Beethoven's *Pastoral* Symphony and Mendelssohn's March for Two Bassoons.

Concepts:

1. The contrabassoon is the lowest instrument in the orchestra.
2. The Italian and German words for a bundle of wood are *fagotto* and *fagott*.

Activities
&
Directions

1. Just for fun, how many other words with *bass* can your students come up with? Using dictionaries and encyclopedias is fine. To the ones they find, add:

Bassano—a walled town in Italy

Bassano Dam—a dam on the Bow River in the province of Alberta, Canada

Bassein—Capital of Irrawaddy—a division of Lower Burma —*good for laughs!*

Basses-Alpes—southeastern section of France, bordering on Italy

2. Beethoven made the bassoon particularly famous and "clownish" by using it to depict the gyrations of an inebriated musician of the village band, in his *Pastoral* Symphony. Mendelssohn wrote a March for two bassoons which delineates the antics of two clowns. As we have said, because it is so often called upon to play comedy roles, the bassoon is sometimes referred to as the clown or comedian of the orchestra. In addition to those we mentioned, use any recordings you can obtain of bassoon concertos or sonatas, to illustrate the comical—and more serious—aspects of the instrument.

3. Among the words "found funny" by many children is *Contrabass sarrusophone*. It certainly is as much a comedian as the bassoon itself. To make your students laugh, use it as a tongue twister. Have them say it over, quickly, five or six times! It is a double-reed, wind instrument, having a conical bore, made of metal and played by a key system similar to that on a saxophone. It was invented in 1865 (the same year that Charles Joseph Sax died!) by Sarrus, a French army bandmaster. As with the saxophones, there is a complete family consisting of six members from the "baby" soprano to the "grandpa" contrabass. As another enjoyable activity, you might want to have younger pupils play the saxophone "family" and the sarrusophone "family" as a type of game. (You be the baby . . . etc. . .)

4. In the lower grades, children enjoy rhyme schemes. Why not try some of these to make up some songs: (You might get a belly laugh or two.)

bassoons
spoons
moons
goons
swoons
tunes
ruins

5. Your scientifically minded students (whose ears perked up when you used the term "conical bore"?) might be interested in the fact that there is also an organ stop called bassoon. Although the large 16-foot pipe is normally called the Contrabassoon or the Contrafagotto

(*chuckle*), Ernest Skinner built a 32-foot (!) Contrafagotto for the Pedal Division of the Woodworth Memorial Organ in the Chapel of Princeton University.

FLUTE FLUTTER

Grades: 2 - 8

Materials: Pictures of flutes and flute players; recorder, songflute, or flutophone.

Concepts:

1. The woodwind family consists of the oboe, bassoon, clarinet, and the flute (even though the flute is now made of metal).
2. The modern flute is transverse or horizontal, as opposed to the recorder, songflute, tonette, or flutophone.

**Activities
&
Directions**

1. Go "brrrr." Have your students go "brrrr." If you were doing this with the flute, this would be called flutter tonguing. Going "brrr" (either by you or your pupils) is a sound that will make your class smile. As with other "funny sounds," the idea is to use them as a point of departure for acquiring some information or gaining a skill. The sound is the motivating factor. A real tickler, teaser, tongue twister is to try to say, quickly, five or six times:

   flute flutter fun
   flute flutter fun
   flute flutter fun
   flute flutter fun
   flute flutter fun

2. Here are some facts for your scientifically minded older students. In ancient and medieval times, the flute was made of wood and consisted of a conical tube into which the performer blew through a mouthpiece located at the upper end; the body of the instrument had holes along its length which were stopped by the fingers to produce the various notes. This type, which can even be made for a Science Fair in your school, is known as the end-blown flute; because of its use in England from 1400-1700, it became known as the English flute. It survives today chiefly in the form of the recorder, songflute, flutophone, or tonette.

3. For the skill component of this lesson, why not get some songflutes or flutophones? The blowing is very simple (very few students have any trouble) and the A, B, C's are pictured in Figure 18.

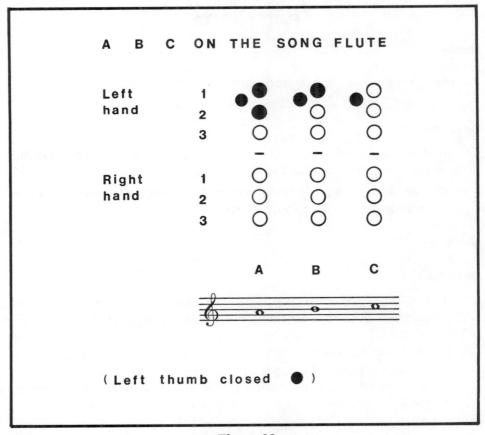

Figure 18

Using A B C, you can teach whole notes (too-oo-oo-oo duration of four counts), half notes (too-oo or two counts), and quarter notes (tah or one count). If interest is maintained, with or without the fun of flute flutter, there are many good method books available to teach a wide variety of familiar tunes. (See Figure 19.)

4. For more fun, did your students know that there is a piping crow known as the flutebird? There are also flutemouths which are marine fish with long cyclindrical snouts classified with (chuckle) pipefishes, sea horses, snipefishes, and sticklebacks.

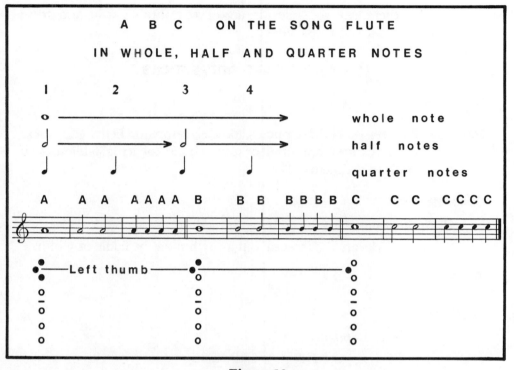

Figure 19

5. What about the flute that you hold sideways, your pupils might be saying? Well, this is known as the transverse flute. (It is also known as the German flute—to distinguish it from the English flute that we discussed earlier.) Flute merely means pipe, of course, and the vertical grooves on Romanesque columns are also called flutes. Sometime in the thirteenth century the side-blown or transverse flute made its appearance, and it soon became preferred over the end-blown flute because its sound projected better. Only in England was the end-blown flute favored.

In the lower grades, why not play Flute Family with your pupils? Look how many there are to choose from. Which one will you be?

flute allemande	flute d'amour
flute a bec	flute, beak
flute discant	flute, english
flute, eunuch	flute, fipple
flute, octave	flute, piccolo

Also, there are kazoos, fifes (are any of your pupils in a fife-and-drum corps?), alto and bass flutes.

CHOPSTICKS AND FIDDLESTICKS

Grades: K - 8

Materials: Pictures of violins, pianos, beetles; resonator bells; chopsticks from a Chinese restaurant or supply house (or actual fiddlesticks if you can get them).

Concepts:

1. Another name for the violin is the fiddle.
2. Fiddlesticks are used to beat out a rhythm on the fiddle or violin.

**Activities
&
Directions**

1. On the chalkboard, write:

> fiddlesticks
> fiddle beetle

A discussion of the fiddle beetle might tickle your pupils. You can explain that it is abundant in Java, it has a slender head and thorax, and a flat abdomen giving the body a shape like that of a violin or fiddle. It is nocturnal. Other "fiddle things" are the fiddler crab or calling crab, and the fiddlefish or guitar fish. Collect and list other "fiddle things" on the chalkboard and on charts around the room.

2. After this background activity, yell out, "Oh fiddlesticks!" See if there is a humorous reaction. The expression is an odd one and not in current usage. You might have to explain that it is, indeed, more than an expression. We have used this little "script" successfully; try reading it dramatically.

> Just an expression you say? No sayest we! Fiddlesticks may have a long history; but they have been used in recent years in the Cayjun (comes from Louisiana French dialect shortened form of Arcadian—arCay-dian—Cay-dian—hence Cay-jiun or Cay-jun) style of playing still seen at folk concerts or concerts that feature bluegrass and other country styles of music.

After the reading, picture a player beating out a rhythm with fiddlesticks on a violin while the violinist or fiddler is playing. Can any of your pupils find real fiddlesticks in an attic or an old trunk? If not, chopsticks from a Chinese restaurant will do. Use a borrowed violin, or invite a violinist to class. Use the chopsticks to play a rhythm on the part of the violin between where the player moves his fingers and where the bow is used.

3. With all this talk of chopsticks, we might add that "Chopsticks" (along with "Heart and Soul") is among the tunes that most children want to learn, according to music teachers surveyed! If a piano is not available, the tune can be played on resonator bells or even a melodica. It simply involves playing sets of notes six times each:

F G		1, 2, 3, 4, 5, 6	F and G six times
E G		1, 2, 3, 4, 5, 6	E and G six times
D	B	1, 2, 3, 4, 5, 6	D and B six times

Next we switch to low C and high C played four times:

C C   1, 2, 3, 4,   (four times)
Finally, two sets are played once each:
D B   (once)
E A   (once)

Let's review, pictorially; to the left or right in Figures 20A and 20B means to the left or right on the piano, melodica, or resonator bells.

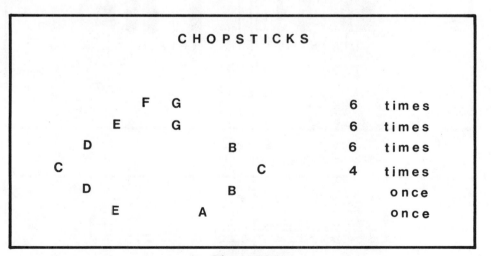

Figure 20A

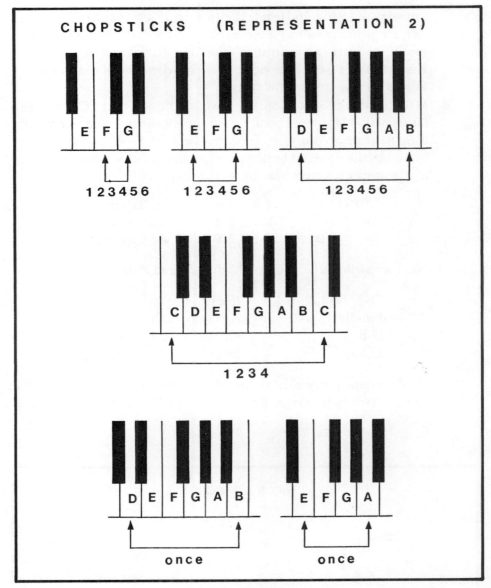

Figure 20B

Figure 20C

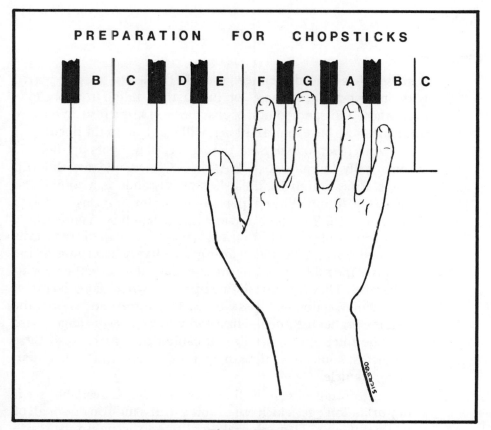

Figure 20D

GLISSANDI

Grades: 3 - 8

Materials: A recording of a full orchestral version of George Gershwin's *Rhapsody in Blue*; rubber bands; large coffee can; wooden box or crate; violin; guitar, ukulele, or a banjo.

Concepts:

1. Members of the string family such as the violin, viola, cello, and bass violin have fingerboards; a glissando is produced by sliding the finger up the fingerboard.

2. The opening of *Rhapsody in Blue* uses a trill and then a glissando on the clarinet.

Activities
&
Directions

1. A *glissando* is defined as either "a very fast scalewise passage played with one finger, i.e., the nail," or, in jazz, the "sliding from one tone to another." Glissandi (plural of glissando) on string instruments are sounds that we have found children will laugh at. In the opening of Gershwin's *Rhapsody in Blue*, the clarinet player goes up the scale chromatically (by half-steps—A, A#, B, C, C#, etc.) and then slides up to the clarinet's high C. This slide or glissando is a sound that children find funny. Why not play this music for your class and see if they are amused? You could also make them laugh by making funny sounds with rubber bands stretched across various sized coffee cans or wooden boxes. The sound you get will vary according to the tightness of the rubber band, its thickness, and the size of the resonating chamber. Then imagine sliding up and down the fingerboards of violins, violas, cellos, and bass violins. The thinner and shorter the string, the higher the pitch—that is why sliding up the fingerboard makes the pitch go higher. If you cannot obtain access to these instruments, you can do the same with the more available guitar, banjo or ukulele.

2. If a piano, portable organ, bell lyra, or melodica is available, see if your pupils don't get a kick out of doing a glissando on one or all of these instruments. They can make a glissando going up the piano with their left thumb nail or with their right middle fingernail. They can effect a glissando going down the piano with their right thumbnail or their left middle fingernail. The secret is to play the glissando lightly on the piano. Some students have found that playing a glissando on the piano can hurt the finger if they dig in too much on the keyboard. Please stress the importance of playing lightly. Mallets can also be used to make a glissando on the bell lyra or on the resonator bells. A glissando on the melodica can be made as on the piano. See if your pupils are not all smiles as they make these glissandi!

WHIPS, WHISTLES, AND WINDMAKERS

Grades: 4 - 8

Materials: Paintings by James Abbott McNeill Whistler, such as *Harmony in Yellow and Gold* or *At the Piano*; various types of parade and penny whistles; a recording of Richard Strauss's *Don Quixote*; popular recordings and recordings of marches using whistles.

Concepts:

1. Richard Strauss's composition, *Don Quixote*, is a tone poem (a musical work telling a story tonally).

2. Whistler, emphasizing the analogy with music, called his paintings arrangements, symphonies, nocturnes, etc.

3. There are many types of whistles that have never been officially in the orchestra's percussion section; whips and windmakers were also added to the percussion section of the orchestra by composers such as Richard Strauss.

Activities
&
Directions

1. Just the thought of a whip being an instrument will make some students laugh! We have found that it is easy to generate a lively discussion about what should and what should not be accepted as an instrument.

2. Listen to Richard Strauss's tone poem, *Don Quixote*. Can you hear the windmaker or wind machine at the point where he is supposed to be fighting windmills?

3. If a piano player is a pianist, and a flute player is a flutist, is a whistle player a whistler or a whistlist? A few giggles are usually elicited by this pun—although most of your pupils will consider it dry or corny. However, a nice discussion or a related arts lesson can be based upon either the snickers or the laughs (whichever they are). You might have your students look at paintings by Whistler and discuss his philosophy of paintings being like frozen music. Are colors like harmonies? Are harmonies like colors? Some musicians claim that they regard certain musical keys as being bright, like certain colors, and others as being soft, like other colors. Younger students can draw to music and give their works Whistler-like titles. Older students can get more involved in whether or not keys in music (scales and harmonies) are like colors.

XYLOPHONES AND BONES

Grades: K - 7

Materials: A recording of Camille Saint-Saëns' *Danse Macabre*; pictures of a xylophone; references to and pictures of a bones player, with his polished bones, if possible.

Concepts:

1. In an old-fashioned minstrel show, along with the actors and dancers there was a tambourine player called "Mr. Tambo," and a bones player called "Mr. Bones."

2. The xylophone is a pitched instrument that is a member of the percussion family. It was used by Saint-Saëns to suggest the rattle of bones in his composition, *Danse Macabre.*

Activities
    &
Directions

1. As background for this lesson, get and polish a large turkey bone, or bones from a cow's leg. You might tell your pupils that this is exactly what "Mr. Bones" did for his part in the minstrel show. He polished up his bones and used them to play rhythms along with "Mr. Tambo," who played his tambourine. Have your own minstrel show—with some of your pupils going "euhh" as you ask them to be "Mr. Bones" and others fighting for the part.

2. In a related activity, older students can list and research the various bones of the body: for example, the radius and ulna of the arm; the tibia and fibula of the leg; and the femur of the thigh. Your scientific geniuses might find it very interesting that bones will carry a greater load than granite or reinforced concrete of equal dimensions, when subjected to stress in the normal direction! Another related activity can be discussing bone fertilizers. Or you can list places such as Bône, a fortified seaport in North Algeria—at the foot of a hill near the Seybouse River.

3. For our "facts" portion of the lesson, students might be interested in hearing that the xylophone was used in ancient orchestras of the orient and in Africa; it was sometimes made of glass on straw and was brought to the attention of the western world by Felix Mendelssohn. In Greek, *xylon* means wood. The modern xylophone is made of wood, is a member of the percussion family of instruments, and is played with mallets with which the musician strikes the hardwood bars that are arranged horizontally on two parallel cords or rubber stands; beneath the bars are resonators that amplify the sound. An electrically amplified xylophone is called a vibraphone. Why not try your hand at making one—it can be fun!

JAWS, JUGS, KAZOOS, HAIRCOMBS
AND
MUSICAL WASHBOARDS

Grades: 2 - 8

Materials: Reccrded "Bluegrass Music"; jaws' harps, kazoos, combs, musical washboards, banjos, fiddles or guitars; recordings and/or pictures of these instruments; thimbles for fingers; knife and/or fork; rubber bands.

Concept:

1. An array of funny sounds comes from instruments used in bluegrass music and other indigenous folk styles.

Activities
&
Directions

1. Once difficult to find, recordings of bluegrass music are becoming increasingly easy to obtain. Students who are not familiar with bluegrass music groups may sometimes find the pictures on the record albums a bit funny. In preparation for such a listening experience, be sure to send your pupils scampering about in attics and garages to look for old tubs and washboards. (If you remember what the washboard looks like, you are showing your age!) Many pupils enjoy this activity.

2. Kazoos and combs are merely blown into, and you change the pitch of your "too-too-too-toos" as you do when singing. The washboard is played with thimbles on your fingers or with the end of a knife or fork. The pitch of the jaws' harp (or Jew's harp) is controlled by the oral cavity, and a free-beating metal tongue is set into motion by striking it with the hand. If your mouth is open wider, the tone is lower; a more closed mouth results in a higher pitch. Many students find the jaws' harp very funny!

3. You can make a monochord by stringing a thick rubber band across a wooden tub (as a resonating chamber). If you tighten the rubber band, the pitch gets higher as you pluck it. A tiny monochord can be made by stretching a rubber band across several manila folders.

JUG BAND

Grades: 3 - 8

Materials: Washboard; thimbles; kazoo; a comb and tissue paper; jugs of various sizes.

Concepts:

1. The term "jug band" is used for a band that plays a type of bluegrass (or folk or Country 'N' Western) music.
2. Children find it fun to create a band with homemade or easy-to-make instruments.

**Activities
&
Directions**

1. Ask your students if they have ever seen a jug band. You might show them pictures or take them to an actual performance if there is one available. We have found that students love to play kazoos or a comb covered with tissue paper. And, once shown how, they find it relatively easy to blow across the top of a jug to produce the various pitches that they can make.
2. Many jug bands use a monochord. A monochord is easy and fun to make. It consists of just one string that can be made from gut, or even rubber bands or plastic—anything that vibrates. The vibrating material is strung across a long board that is attached to a wash basin (which serves as a resonating chamber.) The monochord is then played like a double bass, and the player moves his hand to shorten the string for higher notes. Sometimes, the string is attached to a hole in the bottom of the washbasin. In that case, the long board can be bent or pulled so that the string becomes tighter or looser—higher when it is tighter and lower when it is looser.
3. Cover one or several fingers with thimbles. Now, trying to feel like you're in the Blue Ridge Mountains, make some rhythmic sounds on the washboard, blow across the tops of the jugs, and pluck your homemade monochord. If the sound is not too good, why not play along with some recorded examples of jug band music?

THE BONG OF THE GONG AND BLOCKS

Grades: 3 - 8

Materials: Gong and Chinese temple blocks; mallets; recording of orchestral passage containing a gong; baseball bat; metal garbage can cover. (If an orchestral recording isn't available, use the bat and can cover.)

Concepts:

1. The gong is a non-pitched member of the percussion family.

2. The gong vibrates unevenly and does not have a definite pitch (as do instruments that create a definite primary frequency or fundamental).

3. Chinese temple blocks are percussion instruments of definite pitch. They simulated the sounds of horses' hooves in movies about the wild west.

Activities
&
Directions

1. Another funny sound in an orchestra comes from the gong. If you can't obtain a real gong (they are expensive), take a piece of sheet metal and drill a small hole through the top. Have your bravest pupil come to the front of the classroom to hold the gong suspended by a string, as you prepare to strike it with a mallet. Make believe you are going to hit it real hard and watch your pupil close his eyes!

2. Here is another fun activity. How many times have you heard the sound of Chinese temple blocks without knowing what created the sound? You might have your children simulate this sound by using mouth pops. This merely involves having the child place his finger in his mouth, build up pressure, and then release it with sufficient force to make a pop sound. Most students know exactly what we mean so, you won't have too much explaining to do!

SPOONS AND SAWS

Grades: K - 8

Materials: Spoons and saws.

Concept:

Musical saws and spoons are funny instruments that are likely candidates for traditional folk groups.

Activities
&
Directions

Musical saws and spoons are seen on talent shows where they are a novelty act, as much funny as they are entertaining! Your pupils can do it too, using spoons as drum sticks. (The real spoon player holds two spoons back-to-back so that they hit into each other as the rhythms are played on his knee or the chair he is sitting on.) Sometimes, the spoon player plays on walls or on the floor. The musical saw is even funnier as it emits its plaintive wail, in the hands of an experienced player. We dare you to get a tune on a saw. Just pluck it and bend it to change its pitch, pushing against the floor or a chair. In this way, try creating your own classroom variety show and see if your pupils have fun.

7

More Things Found Funny

"Why are you laughing, Billy?" asked the teacher. "Because it looks so funny," replied the student. This type of conversation occurs frequently when children first see vibrato or ballet dancing. And why not? Children are used to people trying to make them laugh. From being thrown in the air by uncle X to "Punch and Judy" shows or "The Muppets," the more children laugh the better we like it! (In fact, isn't that the case with adult situation comedies, stand-up comedy routines, resort hotel comedians, etc.?) How many of us stay up an extra half-hour or more so we can watch late-night television, making sure not to miss the opening monologue of our favorite talk show host? Included in this chapter are some more things which children find funny—things which we as adults have come to assume are absolutely serious. But are they, really? Are you quite sure they're not still funny to you too?

CRASHING CYMBALS

Grades: K - 4

Materials: Cymbals.

Concepts:

1. The crash of the orchestral cymbals is a sound found funny.
2. The cymbal is found in the percussion section of the orchestra.

Activities
&
Directions

1. Like the bong of the gong, the crash of the orchestral cymbals is a sound found funny. In fact, the younger you are, the funnier this experience is. As soon as very young children stop being scared by loud noises, they begin to find them amusing. This amusement can be enhanced further by directions such as, "cover your ears!" Or, you might try some physical directions such as, "whenever you hear or see the cymbal crash, touch your shoulders, or touch your ankles, or touch your knees." The younger the pupils, the more different parts of the body you can use, even going through all of the fingers with their full and proper names.

2. If at all possible, take your class to see a live concert. The experience of of seeing the cymbals and hearing them is not only louder, there is also the fun of seeing what many music teachers call the "wind up." You see, prior to the actual cymbal crash, the percussionist begins to prepare for it. Sometimes this involves merely looking at the score (the music) and beginning to get sort of nervous; but at other times, the percussionist picks up the cymbals, looks at the conductor, looks back at the score—and then, finally, at just the right moment, crashes the cymbals and then holds them up for full resonance. (Watch how they are held up, pointed at the audience.)

VIBRATO

Grades: K - 5

Materials: Violin and/or guitar; film of a concert orchestra.

Concepts:

1. A player shakes his or her hand to make a string vibrate.
2. Making the string vibrate gives the tone a nicer sound.

Activities
&
Directions

1. "How funny it looks," say many younger pupils when they see *vibrato* for the first time. "Why does that man shake his wrist and his hand? Some giggle outright; others just smile. Nonetheless, it is the exception, rather than the rule, for youngsters first seeing a violinist or a cellist vibrating, to view it seriously. But this humor can be utilized. Children merely have the courage to ask out loud what

many adults want to ask, but are too embarrassed. (After all, past a certain age we are supposed to know everything!)

Best of all, of course, is when students ask questions at, say, a young people's concert where their questions can be answered by a trained professional. If, however, the questions occur during a film, then that means *you* must do the explaining. The definition is not that complicated. You can say: "When a player shakes his or her hand to make the string vibrate, we call it vibrato. Making the string vibrate gives the tone a nicer sound."

2. Another way to begin this lesson is to place the above definition of vibrato on the chalkboard. Of course, you might have to read it to pupils below the fourth grade. Then you might ask the class if they can guess—in the film—where the shaking occurs, or what vibrato is. What does the violinist or cellist do that looks different or funny? At some point during the year, although you should show your class a film of a concert orchestra, try to have a violinist or cellist come to school; or take a trip to a conert hall to attend a live concert.

With an old violin or guitar you obtain, you yourself might demonstrate vibrato. Hold the violin with your left hand (or the guitar if necessary). With your left pointer on one of the strings, pluck the string with your right pointer and then wiggle or slide your left pointer on the string you plucked.

3. For our funny-facts portion of the lesson, lest we think the violin was always the epitome of seriousness, tell your class that in 1627, one of the first pieces conceived in a thoroughly violinistic idiom featured imitations of a dog barking, and of a fife and drum. Called *Cappricio Stravagante*, it was written by Carlo Farina.

OPERATIC SINGING

Grades: K - 5

Material: Tuning fork.

Concept:

When an opera singer sings, the voice box (pharynx) vibrates.

**Activities
&
Directions**

1. Just as a violinist's or cellist's hand trembles or vibrates, so does an opera singer's voice box (pharynx) vibrate. In fact, during television close-ups or when using opera glasses at an opera, one sees the lips

quivering as well. You might explain that this manner is a custom in operatic singing, just as popular music has some customs (purposely using a hoarse, gravelly style of singing, purposely singing flat, etc.). If your students find it funny, use this reaction for an exciting lesson. Comics often satirize operatic singing for comical effects. Do your students know any cartoons that spoof some of the facial mannerisms of opera singers? Will any of your more outgoing pupils come up to the front of your classroom to clasp their hands and make believe they are an opera singer?

Will any of your students laugh if you use the term "fish-mouth?" The word is actually used to describe the mannerism of pushing the lips forward to increase the possibility for resonance. Experienced singers always thrust their lips forward, but manage in most cases to look pleasant while they are doing it. Occasionally you will see an inexperienced amateur who looks quite pained, making the visual impression even more comical.

2. Here is another activity that can stem from this lesson. Take a common tuning fork and strike it so that it begins to vibrate. The tone will be almost inaudible although you can hear it by holding it close to your ear. Then, place the handle of the tuning fork on a desk or the chalkboard right after vibration has begun, and you will hear a clear, mellow tone, often quite loud (because the desk or board is supplying resonance and amplification).

As another related activity, you might also tell your students about the other resonating chambers of the throat, nose, roof of the mouth, tongue, and soft palate; and how the nose, frontal sinuses, and other cavities of the head act as resonating chambers. We have had interesting lessons on how the resonating chambers are supported by the chest cavity, lungs, and the diaphragm.

3. Here is more fun. You know how professional singers walk around going *mee-mee-mee-mee-mee*, or *ay-ee-ah-oh-ooh*? Why not have your class do it, making believe they are famous opera singers. Explain that these sounds are used to introduce nasal resonance. Explain that when someone talks through his nose, we really mean that the nose is blocked up and has stopped the steady flow of the tone through its openings. This is what happens when you have a "code in your dose" (cold in your nose).

Many classes enjoy exercises that are used by (our now accepted?) operatic singers to relax the throat—even for talking. Sing *nee-nay-ee-ay-ee* on different tones or notes going up the scale. To include the upper head cavities, sing the syllable *beu* (as in beautiful) very softly and as high as your range will permit, until you get a definite feeling of vibration in your forehead between the eyes. Explain to your pupils that going through this exercise with plenty of nasal resonance will make the voice clear, and will allow it to carry. It will have a clear quality, and you won't get voice strain as easily.

4. Try these satires on funny operatic customs:

   a. Lean on a piano with the hands clasped together as in a prayer position;

   b. Make assorted funny facial expressions as if trying to get the best possible resonance; move your eyebrows to make it more comical;

   c. Use funny foreign pronunciations such as "goood Evenink Frrreends."

OPERATIC PLOTS

Grades: 3 - 8

Materials: A book giving operatic plots. (Opera Guides or Adventures in Opera).

Concepts:

1. Purposely comical operas are known as *opera comique* (French), *opera buffa* (Italian), *singspiel* (German), and musical comedy (English-American).

2. *Opera seria* and Grand Opera may also have plots that are unintentionally comical.

**Activities
&
Directions**

1. Operatic plots are often funny, even when they are not meant to be. For example, in Rigoletto, as we mentioned earlier, Gilda pops out of a sack and—although she has just been murdered—sings for a while before finally succumbing. In another opera, the poor hero has to sing a long passage with a spear sticking between his shoulder blades and presumably into his lungs. In two other operas, the sopranos, both dying of tuberculosis, sing for quite a while on their deathbeds! In another instance, the hero's finger is heated along with the blood of a slain giant dragon. As he unwittingly puts his finger to his lips to cool it he tastes the blood, and thus learns the language of the birds. So absurd are plots like these that the philosopher Scho-

penhauer defined opera as an unmusical invention for the pleasure of unmusical people. And, in an essay by John Dryden, he observed that "... in all our tragedies, the audience cannot forbear laughing when the actors are about to die."

2. Ask your class, "Was Schopenhauer right? Is opera unmusical? What about well-liked operas such as *Porgy and Bess* or *Carmen*?" Use your opera guide or plot book to go over plots that are absurd and ridiculous, and ones that are not weird or comical in any way.

3. Another interesting activity is to write opera plots of two types: ones that are purposely comical and/or weird; and ones that are serious and sad in every way.

4. Many music teachers have found that they could capitalize on the energy generated by laughing at genuinely and intentionally funny operas, as well as opera plots found funny although they were not meant to be so. Many of Wagner's operas, based upon German folklore, have plots that are hilariously funny. Rossini wrote many comic operas or *opera buffi*. Both of these composers can be studied in greater detail; after the initial fun of laughing *at* them, we can proceed to laughing *with* them and, then, to enjoying the music itself.

5. A *libretto* is the text or play for an opera, usually with the original language on the left and the English translation on the right. Teach this fact to your pupils. Then have your pupils write a new libretto for an opera of your choice. They can also take an original story, or a fairy tale, and write a libretto for it.

6. Younger pupils love to act out roles from some of the more funny operas, or the funny passages from operas not considered funny by some opera-goers. Perhaps they can be Figaro from *The Barber of Seville*, which Rossini wrote with words by Sterbini (based on Beaumarchais's comedy). Or they can be Papageno from Mozart's *The Magic Flute.* Here are two scenes children love:

   a. Count Almaviva uses an alias—Count Lindoro. Competing for Rosina's love with her ward, Dr. Bartolo, Almaviva /Lindoro sneaks into the house disguised as a drunken dragoon, then disguised as a music teacher. As a drunken dragoon he is arrested; but as a music teacher he gains admission and woos Rosina.

   b. Papageno lies, and claims that he has killed a serpent that was chasing him. As punishment, three attendants of the queen, who really killed it themselves, place a padlock on his mouth; but he keeps trying to speak!

CONDUCTOR'S HAIR BOBBING UP AND DOWN

Grades: 1 - 6

Materials: A wig; a baton; most classical recordings.

Concept:

The leader of an orchestra is called the conductor.

Activities
&
Directions

1. It used to be more fashionable to call serious musicians "longhairs." That is because, while most men wore their hair short, composers and orchestra conductors wore their hair long (perhaps originally because they couldn't afford haircuts). One result was that when the conductor got very engrossed in the music and/or very excited, his hair used to bob up and down. When seeing this for the first time, many pupils find it very funny. If you have a film library in your school, you might want to look through it, to see if any films of the orchestra have a portion where the conductor's hair does bounce a bit. Then see what your class's reaction is.

2. You might try having a student who is an extrovert do some conducting with a baton and a wig (store bought or made from paper). He can purposely make the wig bob up and down excessively—for an extra comical effect!

SHAKING, WEAVING, KNITTING, ROWING AND STIRRING

Grades: 1 - 8

Concept:

In order to get an orchestra to play different ways, some conductors make funny gestures.

Activities
&
Directions

Along with the hair bobbing up and down, there are other funny gestures which conductors have. Some of them make children laugh some of the time. When they are exaggerated, most children will laugh! With some exciting classical music of your choice, you and your students exaggerate the following gestures:

 a. when some really exciting musical passages are played, the make-believe conductor starts shaking violently;
 b. when the music is a little more quiet, a weaving motion is used;
 c. for other passages of fairly quiet music, a knitting motion can be simulated;
 d. a rowing motion can be used when the music starts to "take off" again;
 e. a stirring movement can be used in sections which are a little more turbulent but not as energetic as those parts for which you did the shaking gesture.

CATGUT AND HORSEHAIR

Grades: 1 - 6

Materials: A violin and a bow; rosin.

Concepts:

 1. Violin strings always used to be made from catgut.
 2. A violin bow always used to use horsehair.

**Activities
 &
Directions**

 1. You might start this lesson by standing in front of your classroom with a violin in your hand; or you can start putting rosin (pronounced rah-zin) on a violin bow. The correct way of putting the rosin on is by holding the rosin with your right hand and rubbing it on the bow. Some players still prefer to rub the bow (held with the right hand) onto the rosin. Don't be worried if the rosin doesn't appear to go onto the bow; sometimes it has to be "started" by scratching it with a pin or your nail. This should get the class's attention and they'll start asking you what you are doing. If you can get some scratchy sounds or squeaks, you and your class can start having some fun. You might want to review the lesson on the glissando, or you may need a beginning violin book to show you how to hold the violin and the bow. Your students can have fun trying to get some sounds (or squeaks) out of the instrument. Oh

well, they can always play it *pizzicato* which means plucking the strings and not using a bow.

2. Now for even more fun. Unfortunately these days, so many things are made from synthetic fibers. Until fairly recently, all violin strings were made from catgut; and all violin, viola, cello, and double bass bows used horsehair. This fact, considered amusing by music teachers, was conveyed to students—who usually outdid their teachers in being amused (catgut? *eeuhh, yuch* horsehair? *yipes*).

3. Older pupils can explore this subject in greater detail, perhaps writing a research report on synthetic fibers. Nowadays the bows are made with nylon and other synthetics. The strings are often steel, or steel wound around other fibers. This might even lead to research into how the violin is made and its history.

NO APPLAUSE YET

Grades: 4 - 8

Materials: None or concert programs.

Concepts:

1. It is a sometimes-found-funny fact in music that it is bad protocol to applaud between the movements of a symphony or concerto.

2. It is also funny to some children that music is one of the few arts in which the performers are given applause before they do anything.

Activities
&
Directions

1. One activity that is fun is for an outgoing student to play being the conductor. When he comes out of "the wings," the rest of the pupils who are acting as the audience give the student-conductor a great deal of applause—perhaps a standing ovation. A discussion can ensue about why this is done. Except for very big stars, actors are not applauded before they finish a performance. Why is the conductor applauded as he comes to the podium? Why are the members of a quartet applauded as they come out on the stage? With smiles on their faces, children have asked us this many times. You might explain that this is a custom or tradition. Or you might compare it to famous rock or disco stars coming out on the stage. You might even assign some students to research this tradition.

2. Students have also asked why they can't applaud between the movements of a symphony. You can reply to this question that it breaks the conductor's concentration and, because of this courtesy, someone who applauds between movements of the symphony might get dirty looks from other members of the audience! Thus, it is easier to follow protocol than to try to change it. It is a lot of fun to play applauding at the wrong time and getting the necessary dirty looks from other members of the audience.

ALL ORCHESTRAS SOUND ALIKE WARMING UP

Grades: 4 - 8

Materials: Tuning forks or water glasses of different sizes; a film of an orchestra.

Concepts:

1. The term "warming up" means just that for the wind instruments, and often is used jointly with the expression "tuning up."
2. Pitch (highness of lowness) is determined by vibrations-per-second (v.p.s.).

**Activities
&
Directions**

1. Write on the chalkboard, or ask your pupils:

WHY DO ALL ORCHESTRAS SOUND ALIKE
WHEN TUNING UP? WARMING UP?

The answer is quite simple. The oboe sounds a pitch known as *concert A* (which is 440 v.p.s. or vibrations-per-second) soon after the wind players have had a chance to warm up their instruments. You can explain that, if the instruments are not warm, brasses and woodwinds tend to be flat. After the oboe plays the concert A, the strings and other instruments immediately tune up to this tone, to see whether they are "in tune," "flat," or "sharp." What does "in tune," "flat," and "sharp" really mean, your students might ask? Can you explain it to them? Why are so many student orchestras "flat"? Well, "in tune" means that the vibrations-per-second of one instrument are almost exactly the same as those of another instrument. "Flat" means that a pitch has fewer vibrations-per-second, making it slightly lower than one that is "in tune." "Sharp" means slightly higher or more vibrations-per-second. Using the concert A pitch of 440 v.p.s., for example, a pitch that is "flat" might be 337 v.p.s.; a pitch that is "sharp" might be 443 v.p.s.

2. For some reason, the sound of an orchestra tuning and warming up is amusing to children. See if you can discover why.

3. Another activity related to pitch uses water glasses. They are partially filled to different levels, thus giving them different pitches. The larger the glass and/or the less water in it, the lower the pitch or sound. Your pupils can make a scale by using the larger glasses for the lower notes and the smaller glasses for the higher notes (see Figure 21). If you have only glasses of the same size, put in less water for the lower notes.

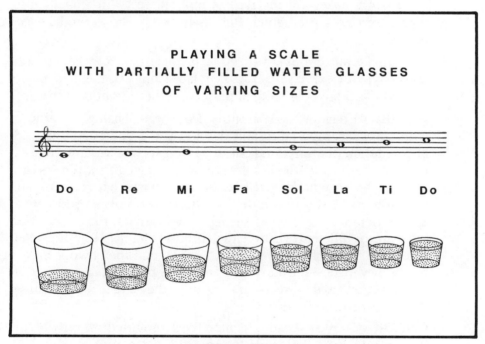

Figure 21

SWANS AND OTHER FUNNY BALLET CUSTOMS

Grades: 1 - 5

Materials: Pictures of ballet dancers; action pictures of hockey, football and baseball games; pictures of boxers.

Concept:

Sports motions and poses often resemble dance movements.

**Activities
&
Directions**

1. The great actor Walter Slezak (whose father was a great Wagnerian opera singer) wrote a book called, *What Time Is the Next Swan?* It satirized many of the funny ballet-in-opera customs, one of them being the cluster of dancers who are moving their arms and legs in swan-like fashion. Nowadays, even famous choreographers themselves satirize funny ballet movements. (See Chapter 5, first lesson, Activity 3.)

2. Contrast some strong close-fisted movements with ones where the open hand makes a flying type of motion. See which ones cause giggles or outright laughter. Purposely exaggerate to produce the desired effect.

3. Try to get some of your boys to go up on their toes; note the "are you crazy" type of expressions on their faces; but ask them to move around like a boxer or football player and they might be pleased.

4. Now that we have derided the outmoded aspects of ballet, it is time to emphasize its importance and develop some understanding and appreciation. Like anything else, it has its excesses. You might need to go more into football, baseball, and basketball movements to compare how any art form reflects the times in which it exists. We are sure you will have no trouble in getting your boys to simulate a hockey or football game. But then, can they turn it into a dance? And what are the differences between a dance and a game? How did ballet reflect the times of the Court of LouisXIV and the bowing movements they made—the movements that they had to make because of the dress they used to wear—and the dress they had to wear because there was no central heating?

5. Contrast movements made down on the floor with those only up in the air. Why didn't ballet use the floor? Why does modern dance?

TOY INSTRUMENTS

Grades: K - 4

Materials: A recording of Haydn's *Toy* Symphony; comb and tissue paper; toy piano; toy drums; recorders; kazoos, ocarina; candy whistle; trombone flute.

Concepts:

1. Toy instruments contain some of the fundamentals of actual instruments.

2. Toy instruments can be bought or made; some are games.

**Activities
&
Directions**

1. Play Haydn's *Toy* Symphony. Have your pupils raise their hands whenever they think they hear a toy instrument. Some teachers have their students stand up—others have pupils write slash marks. Our pupils have often done drawings of what they hear in Haydn's music, both traditional instruments and the ones that are toys.

2. A toy drum may seem funny to students who don't want to be treated like or considered babies. But, a toy drum can easily lead to a real one, and you can discover children's musical talents by how they play with musical toys. Let your students play with whatever toy instruments you can buy, borrow, beg for, and find in old attics and trunks. They can act as stimuli for work with both easy-to-play instruments such as song flutes, Swiss Melode Bells, or resonator bells, and with instruments they will learn to play later on such as clarinets and trumpets. The students who are fascinated with toy trumpets or saxophones may later make it their business to play them. "Play with them now and, later, you will play them," you can say.

3. Another activity is to make toy instruments and real instruments. A drum can be made from any sort of tin can or wooden box. Look at the assortment of steel drums that abound in the Caribbean! Children can make small xylophones out of wooden slabs knocked out of soapboxes (where you can still find them). A "bottle organ" can be made from glass bottles of various sizes—the different sizes produce a variety of pitch as do musical glasses. They can be tied together and then the player blows across their tops to produce a funny sound. Many pupils are amused by the pitch getting higher and lower as they move to the left or the right blowing across the tops of the bottles. Other musical toys can be studied to see how they are made and if they can be duplicated.

FOUND FUNNY FINALE

Here are some briefer ticklers that can be used during shorter periods.

1. Ask your pupils, "Did you know that they used to have records to teach canaries to sing?"

2. Show cartoons that children find funny and listen carefully to the sound track. Cartoons make greater use of classical music than most other types of movies.

3. Place some "funny terms" from old jazz on the chalkboard or posters:

    ALLIGATOR — follower of swing
    BOILERS — large drums
    CATS — hot musicians
    DOG HOUSE— bass fiddle
    LONG HAIR — classical musician
    PLUMBER — trumpeter
    SQUEAKBOX — violin
    WOODPILE — xylophone

4. Tell your students about some of the instruments of so-called 20th century "serious music":

    BOXING GLOVES — used to play the Harry Partch giant marimba
    RADIOS PLAYING STATIC — used by John Cage

5. What about the anvil (in Verdi's "Anvil Chorus")? Should that be thought of as an instrument? How about a cannon (Tchaikovsky's *1812* Overture)? Should that be thought of as an instrument?

Name That Tune

8

People have made as much as $128,000 merely for knowing the correct title of a song! It is a universal game that people love to play—and the same is true for your students. Included in this chapter are ideas for using television themes; radio and television commercials; the so-called "top 40" popular recordings that children spend so much time listening to; songs that are about animals or have animals in the title; songs about cities; songs about states; national anthems and songs associated with other countries; songs about mountains and rivers; and songs with similar rhythms. We have tried to capitalize on the aspect of games and puzzles that children love—and the natural competitiveness between boys and girls or between students who have slightly differing tastes. Taste can't be taught but it can be caught! Tricks can do more to build bridges to understanding than a rigid, uncompromising attitude about what students want to hear when they are alone without adults! When was the last time you associated Morse code with music? We bet you will have fun with this activity.

ENERGIZER AND WARM-UP

Grades: 1 - 8

Materials: A recording of or music for "America the Beautiful."

Concept:

Musical concepts can be learned from jokes about songs.

Activities
     &
Directions

Since we are going to be naming tunes in this chapter, perhaps we should also focus a bit on some of the words of songs we know. Using the song "America the Beautiful," can you and your students think of any variations on the following teaser?

Question: "Why is "America the Beautiful" like the C Major Scale?

Answer: Because it goes from C to C ("... from Sea to shining Sea"). Get it?

Of course we and other music teachers have gotten the response that this is corny. But, please be assured that when students are asked to write their own joke on C to C (C, D, E, F, G, A, B, C), what they come up with is quite similar. For example,

Teacher: "Why is 'America the Beautiful' like the C Major Scale?"

Student: "I don't know."

Teacher: "Because the C Major Scale goes from C to C; see?"

Student: "Si!"

You might find this warm-up better if your class knows the song. Have you forgotten it? Just in case, here is the first stanza.

> *Oh beautiful for spacious skies*
> *For amber waves of grain*
> *For purple mountain majesty*
> *Above the fruited plain*
> *America, America, God shed His grace on thee*
> *And crowned thy good with brotherhood*
> *From sea to shining sea.*

Finally, since this chapter is called "Name That Tune," the warm-up can be written as follows:

Teacher: "Which song goes from C to C like the C Major Scale?"

Student: (Shrugs) "I don't know. Which one?"

Teacher: " 'America The Beautiful,' because it goes 'from sea to shining sea'."

NAME THAT TUNE

Grades: 2 - 8

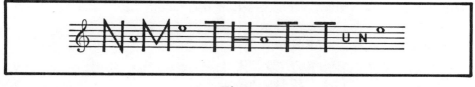

Figure 22

Materials: Music flash cards (not essential).

Concepts:

1. When reading the G clef, E can be either on the first (bottom) line or on the fourth space (from the bottom).

2. A whole note is written like a circle and gets four beats in common time (4/4).

Activities
&
Directions

1. As another warm-up for this chapter, place Figure 22 on the chalk-board or on music flash cards. Ask your students if they can figure out the letter names of the music notes in the diagram. If they figure out that the first note is "A," they should be able to recognize the first word, *name*. Younger students can be asked questions such as, "How did you know the second word was *that*? or that the third word is *tune*?" Such questions might be inappropriate for your older pupils.

2. Older children can also learn that all the notes drawn in Figure 22 are whole notes and will get four beats in common or 4/4 time. You might want them to go *ta-a-a-a-*, to avoid their thinking that the four beats are separate sounds. (The four beats are four beats duration.)

MOON-JUNE-SPOON-TUNES

Grades: 2 - 8

Concept:

Children love rhyme much of the time. They can often engage in simple, creative acts.

Activities
&
Directions

1. There are many, many tunes that were written in the 1920's and

1930's with rhyme schemes that use *moon, tune,* and *June.* For example,

> *By the light,*
> *Of the silvery moon,*
> *I want to spoon,*
> *With my honey in June*
>
> or
>
> *Shine on, shine on harvest moon*
> *Up in the sky*

Can your pupils create two more lines that rhyme? Why not see if they can play "Name That Tune" with songs that have *June,* or *moon,* or *spoon* in them.

2. Younger students might prefer—or be more capable—of rhyming words. For example,

Noon   Goon   Room
Croon   Swoon   Boom

We feel that this is the beginning of creativity. You might want to tell your students that there is a song by George Gershwin that goes.

> *Blah, blah, blah, blah moon*
> *Blah, blah, blah, blah spoon,*
> *Blah, blah, blah, blah, croon*
> *Blah, blah, blah, blah, June*

TELEVISION THEMES

Grades: 3 - 8

Materials: Television guides (*TV Guide* or ones from newspapers and shopping centers); cassette tape recorder and blank tapes.

Concepts

We can capitalize on natural enthusiasm for background music.

Activities
&
Directions

Record opening themes from television programs on a cassette player. Bring them to class and ask your pupils to name them. You might want to list possible answers on the chalkboard. If funds permit it, you might choose to record some of the musical themes on separate tapes, to permit individualized listening experiences. Some teachers like to choose up sides and see which side guesses more than the other—sort of harnessing competition in this game—for more fun! Other teachers make the titles of the programs into puzzles and word games. Still others use this variant: students use television guides to circle names of programs that they want you to record; you then record the musical themes and bring them to class. Don't worry—although they are all requested themes, there will be some errors as the children hear the music without the usual, visual stimulus.

TELEVISION THEMES #2

Grades: 3 - 7

Materials: A recorded portion of a favorite television program, or its opening theme; paper and pencil for writing a script.

Concepts:

1. Most pupils have favorite programs they enjoy watching on television.
2. When a television theme stimulates the brain, one soon envisions the program itself.

Activities
&
Directions

What a marvelous opportunity for acting out a part of a television program! We hear so much about related arts and arts education that we often forget how very basic it is to children to imitate their favorite actors and actresses or to want to be exactly like them. Using a recorded portion of a favorite television program, or its opening theme, ask your pupils to reenact their favorite scene from the program series. Soon after they have decided what their favorite scene is, try to motivate them to write their own script, making minor modifications but giving it a distinctive profile. One simple, basic change can be merely changing names.

Once the scenes have been improvised, and later when you have written scripts, you can play "Name That Tune." How? Have the more assertive students read these scripts. Then, ask other students, who have not written any, to try to name the programs and/or sing the musical themes used for the programs. We have found this to be a very worthwhile activity that weds music and drama very nicely—and permits a lot of fun!

COMMERCIALS

Grades: 2 - 7

Materials: Pre-recorded television themes; tape recorder.

Concepts:

1. Musical themes of commercials heard on television can be used to play games in school.
2. Contests are fun.

**Activities
&
Directions**

A lesson similar to the one on television themes can be created with radio and television commercials. Pre-record ones you have selected or which your pupils themselves have suggested. Then have a contest to see who can guess the most. One way to play the game is to divide the class into teams.

Another way to play the game is to have a quiz show with two contestants, or two families of contestants. Your host for the show might have had to create the tapes himself (so he could know the titles best).

Some music teachers have found that the most effective tapes are ones of commercials that are funny. Extra fun can be had by trying to create your own out-takes or bloopers. You might re-record some, purposely using slips of the tongue or plays on words.

TOP 40

Grades: 3 - 8

Materials: A portable record player; a thick batch of the latest 45 RPM recordings of the top pop groups.

Concepts:

1. The top 40 popular tunes are usually well known by most students, and can be used to develop music listening skills.
2. The diversity in taste for popular music has been created because there are many different types on the market.

Activities
&
Directions

Any experienced teacher in the field knows the appeal of the so-called top 40 or the top 10, and since the advent of the transistor radio, it is difficult to keep them out of the classroom. Why not capitalize on this enthusiasm? Why not harness this energy rather than fight it? As many music teachers have done, simply get used to the fact that top pop can be the vehicle through which listening skills will be developed.

The procedure or game plan involves asking your students to bring in their favorite popular recordings. The game is played by students seeing if they can name each others' recordings. Of course, they will be able to more easily if most of the students have the same recordings. However, this is not always the case. Increasingly, there are so many types of popular music that tastes vary. When this is the case, a lively debate will ensue as to what is the best type of music. Don't be overly concerned if this debate is more heated than you want it to be. First, it is healthy when students love their music so much that they are willing to argue about its merits. Second, this strength of conviction can be structured. It can be utilized in a formal debate where you choose up sides and eventually have a winner. Prizes can be given out, as is done on the increasing number of game programs on television.

ANIMAL SONGS

Grades: K - 8

Materials: Recordings of (or words and music for): (1) songs about animals such as, "Mary Had a Little Lamb," "Old MacDonald," "Baa Baa Black Sheep," "How Much is that Doggy in the Window," or "We Are Siamese if you Please"; and (2) Songs with Animals in the title such as, "Hold That Tiger" or "Tiger Rag," "Alley Cat Song," "What's New Pussycat?" "Hound Dog," or "Baby Elephant Walk."

Concepts:

1. Playing "Name That Tune" can be fun.
2. Children like songs about animals.

**Activities
&
Directions**

1. Younger students can "Name That Tune" by hearing you sing some of the songs to them, or hearing you play the songs on a phonograph and then telling you the title. Pupils who are just learning to write love writing on the chalkboard; why not have them write the title on the board right after you sing a song or play it? To them, writing is fun! Other recordings can be obtained and these titles can be listed on the chalkboard.

Jaws	Talk to the Animals
Wolverine Blues	The Lion Sleeps Tonight
Born Free	Peter Cottontail
The Chipmunk Song	The Donkey Serenade
Rudolph the Red-Nosed Reindeer	

2. For older students, you might want to try songs that use animal titles and animal sounds but which really have political overtones and double meanings. Some examples are, "Three Blind Mice," "Little Piggies," and "White Rabbit." These songs can be sung or listened to. After placing the titles on the board, you can have your students volunteer to sing them or to bring in a recording.

3. Musical concepts can also be extracted from animal songs—as from any type of songs. Place Figure 23 on the chalkboard or on music flash cards.

WHIFFENPOOF SONG

Figure 23

Explain that Figure 23 starts with a G clef ♦ , continues with three flats ♭ ♭ ♭, and then uses the time sign or time signature of 3/4. The note values used, you can continue to say, are quarter, eighth, half and dotted half notes. These are shown in Figure 24.

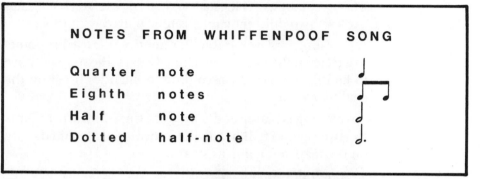

Figure 24

You can also explain or simply state the durations or number of counts for each of the notes used in Figure 23, "The Whiffenpoof Song."

type of note	number of counts
quarter note	— 1
eighth note	— ½ or 2 to a count
half note	— 2
dotted half note	— 3

(If this is too much like hard work, remember our motto: have fun when you get the job done!)

SONGS ABOUT CITIES

Grades: 3 - 8

Materials: Recordings of (or words and music for) songs about cities such as, "I Love New York," "New York, New York, A Wonderful Town," "My Kind of Town" (which is about Chicago), or "By the Time I Get to Phoenix"; map of the United States.

Concepts:

1. Songs about cities are a good way to teaching and learning geography in addition to music.

2. Songs about cities help teach listening skills.

Activities
&
Directions

1. Using a map of the United States, your students can learn where cities mentioned in songs are located, and, of course, in which states they are. At least two different games can be played with this idea:

   a. A recording is played and at the same time the teacher points to a state on the map of the United States; the students have to find the correct city according to the titles listed on the chalkboard; or,

   b. A recording is played and at the same time the teacher points to a title on the chalkboard; the students have to find the city on the map and name its state.

2. Additional song titles you can use are:

Do You Know What it Means to Miss New Orleans ?	— Louisiana
I Left My Heart In San Francisco	— California
Meet Me In St. Louis	— Missouri
On the South Side of Chicago	— Illinois
The Cincinnati Kid	— Ohio
Charleston	— South Carolina
Wabash Cannonball	— Tennessee
Kansas City	— Missouri
Miami Beach Rhumba	— Florida
Hooray For Hollywood	— California
On the Boardwalk in Atlantic City	— New Jersey

SONGS ABOUT STATES

Grades: 3 - 8

Materials: A map of the United States: a good phonograph; and recordings of (or words and music for) some of the songs listed below.

Back Home In Indiana	Moonlight In Vermont
Nothing Could Be Finer Than To Be In Carolina In the Morning	Sweet Home Alabama
California Here I Come	Oklahoma
Beautiful Ohio	Georgia On My Mind

Stars Fell on Alabama   Memphis Tennessee
                                            (Chuck Berry)
        Missouri Waltz   Tennessee Waltz

Concept:

Songs about states can be used to learn geography of the United States

**Activities
        &
Directions**

1. Songs about states may be even more numerous than ones about
    cities. Puzzles can be made with the titles. And the same types of
    games can be played as with the previous lesson on "Songs About
    Cities." Be sure to have students find the states described in songs on a
    map of our country. Another activity is to have a spelling bee using
    the song titles.

2. Can you and your pupils find any other songs about states? Are there
    states without a state song (or a pep song for a leading state college)?
    If there are, perhaps you and your students can embark upon the
    creative activity of writing one. Naturally, any music you may think
    of should be written down; but you can also use a tape recorder. We
    have found that pupils are eager to make up their own songs and be
    real composers. Let us know if you have a similar experience.

Still another activity applies Morse code to music. Eighth notes (which
frequently go quickly) can be represented by *dots* (•) and the quarter notes or
notes still slower can be represented by dashes (–). Let us see how this can be
applied to "Beautiful Ohio." Place Figure 25 on the chalkboard or music
flash cards.

"BEAUTIFUL OHIO"

Figure 25

Call attention to the number 24 at the beginning. This merely means that there are twenty-four measures prior to where we have selected the excerpt from the song. Since this song is in 3/4 time, the twenty four measures of rest would be counted as follows: ONE two three, TWO two three, THREE two three, and so on and so forth up until TWENTY-FOUR two three.

The conversion of music to Morse code might be represented in the following fashion (see Figure 26):

```
    B E A U T I F U L    O H I O    R H Y T H M S

       Beau-ti-ful  O-hi-o  in

         •       •      —     —     —     —

         f       f      s     s     s     s
         a       a      l     l     l     l
         s       s      o     o     o     o
         t       t      w     w     w     w
```

Figure 26

After this example, you and your pupils can play "Name That Tune" by making other examples using Morse code.

NATIONAL ANTHEMS

Grades: 2 - 8

Materials: Recordings of national anthems, a globe or a world map.

Concept:

Singing national anthems of the world can be used to teach world geography, customs of different countries.

**Activities
&
Directions**

Arousing and stimulating! Exciting! These are adjectives that have been associated with the French national anthem ("La Marseillaise"). And we certainly know that our national anthem, "The Star-Spangled Banner," and the Canadian national anthem, "O, Canada," have the capacity to make our spines tingle and our eyes tear at the proper moment. As with songs about cities and states, anthems can be a delightful way of learning geography. You might want to sew or construct traditional costumes or dress, depending on the particular anthems you were able to obtain. Some national anthems require small touches only. For example, a beret might be enough to conjure up a vision of or allude to France; a maple leaf refers to Canada; a bowler hat can make us think of England, and a kilt calls to mind Ireland or Scotland.

When playing "Name That Tune" with recorded examples of national anthems, the titles listed on the board will be one way of making the game easier; another way is to use costumes or other visual hints. For example, if playing the little-known Turkish national anthem, a student wearing a fez might provide the necessary visual clue to enable the other pupils to make the correct guess. Another correct guess can be made by seeing a ski outfit (if students know or have learned that Switzerland is one of the principal skiing area in the world). The national anthem of Spain might be correctly guessed if travel posters showing pictures of a bullfight are used.

SONGS ASSOCIATED WITH COUNTRIES

Grades: 3 - 8

Materials: Recordings of the following songs, and other instrumental and vocal works that have the names of cities and countries in their titles:

The Warsaw Concerto	— Poland
Goodby to Rome (Arrivederci Roma)	— Italy
Danny Boy (Londonderry Air)	— Ireland
Wonderful Copenhagen	— Denmark
Poor People of Paris	— France

Some tunes have the nations themselves in the title

Mexican Hat Dance	Brazil
Song of India	Swedish Rhapsody

Concept:

There are songs that have the names of foreign cities and foreign countries in their titles.

Activities
&
Directions

Write the titles listed above on the chalkboard. Ask your pupils if they have ever heard any of these songs. For example, students of Irish descent may have heard "Danny Boy." Try to get students to talk about the music (... "my father sings it," or . . . "my mother plays the record a lot when . . ."). Ask if anyone can sing or whistle any of the songs listed on the board. The next step is to play recordings that you or your pupils have brought to school. You don't have to limit yourselves to the ones we have suggested. These are merely some of the many song titles we have collected from other music teachers and teachers such as yourself who have found the activity fun to do. In playing "Name That Tune" you needn't aim for the exact song title. Sometimes, there will be a unique sound or rhythm in the song that will cause immediate recognition of the country of origin, or the country the song alludes to. The sound of an accordion often makes us think of Paris. A conga drum often makes us think of the Caribbean or African nations. Castenets make us think of Spain.

MOUNTAINS AND RIVERS

Grades: 3 - 8

Materials: Songs about names, flowers, the weather, colors, months, days of the week, foods, and the stars or the sky.

Concept:

Songs are written about almost every aspect of our life and the world around us.

**Activities
&
Directions**

Although we have entitled this lesson "Mountains and Rivers," for short, you can also play "Name That Tune" with many other categories. Eight other categories are listed below: (1) names; (2) flowers; (3) weather; (4) colors; (5) months; (6) days of the week; (7) foods; (8) stars and sky. You play the game by writing the category on the chalkboard, then listing as many songs as you can in each one of them. Then, you and your students bring to school as many recordings as you can. Don't forget to use the public libraries! Many libraries now have branches that have circulating record collections. Remember, our titles are examples you can look for; but you may be able to find many more different songs.

Names

Georgy Girl	Stella By Starlight
Michelle	Delilah
Daisy	Ruby

Mary
Alfie
Sylvia's Mother
Marianne
Laura
Hey Jude
Dolores Waltz
Peggy O'Neil
Mame

Linda
Mandy
Dianne
Maria
Hello Dolly
Suzanne
Eleanor Rigby
Sherry
Rosie

Flowers
Everything's Coming Up Roses
Apple Blossom Time
Yesterday's Gardenias

Days of Wine and Roses
Edelwiss
When You Wore a Tulip

Weather and Seasons
Stormy Weather
Autumn Leaves
Younger Than Springtime
It Might as Well Be Spring

Here's That Rainy Day
Autumn in New York
Spring Is Here
Summertime

Months
September Song
April Love
I'll Remember April

See You in September
April in Paris
June Is Busting Out All Over

Colors
Clockwork Orange
Tie a Yellow Ribbon
Deep Purple
My Blue Heaven
Ballad of the Green Berets
Yellow Submarine
Blue Velvet

Yellow Bird
Red Roses for a Blue Lady
Love Is Blue
Green Dolphin Street
Pink Panther
Blue Moon
Old Black Magic

Days Of The Week
Ruby Tuesday
Thank God It's Friday
Any Wednesday
Come Thursday
Saturday Night Is the
    Loneliest Night of the Week

Rainy Days and Mondays
Never on Sunday
Wednesday's Child
Come Saturday Morning

Stars and Sky
Star Trek Theme
Close Encounters

2001
East Of the Sun

Full Moon and Empty Arms
Polka Dots and Moonbeams
Moonglow
House Of the Rising Sun
Fly Me to the Moon
Shine on Shine on Harvest Moon

I'm Always Chasing Rainbows
Over the Rainbow
Moonlight Bay
Good Morning Sunshine
Moonlight Serenade
Here Comes the Sun

Foods

There's an Awful Lot of Coffee
   in Brazil
Apple Blossom Time
Blueberry Hill
Mares Eat Oats
Shrimp Boats Are Coming
Watermelon Man
Lollypops and Roses
Raisins and Almonds
Life Is Just a Bowl of Cherries
Hot Cross Buns
Milk and Honey
Cockles and Mussels
Peppermint Twist

Parsley, Sage, Rosemary and
   Thyme
Tangerine
Peas Porridge Hot
Tea for Two
Jambalaya
Candy Man
Salt Peanuts
Strawberry Fields Forever
I Heard It Through the Grapevine
Muffin Man
March Of the Sugar Plum Fairies
Lemon Tree
Old Buttermilk Sky

What about "Mountains and Rivers"? Oh well—"Climb Every Mountain," "Down By the Riverside," "Ebb Tide," "Down By the Old Mill Stream," "Red River Valley," "She'll Be Coming Round the Mountain," *Grand Canyon Suite*, "This Land Is Your Land."

SONG TITLES PUZZLE

Grades: 3 - 7

Materials: A rexograph machine; rexograph ditto master.

Concepts:

1. Puzzles can be made using musical song titles as the answers.
2. Puzzles can help teach the meanings of vertical, horizontal, and diagonal.

**Activities
   &
Directions**

Do your pupils enjoy doing puzzles? If they do, this activity can also help them learn song titles. Figure 27 can be placed on a ditto master or drawn on the chalkboard for your students to copy. You might want to first explain (or review) the meanings of the terms vertical, horizontal, and diagonal.

Many teachers have found that pupils enjoy making puzzles themselves. By a simple show of hands you might have your students vote on doing the puzzle we have provided or making up one of their own. We have found that children enjoy a contest as to who can make the best puzzle.

Can you find the following songs in this puzzle? Circle the songs when you find them. They may be read from left to right, right to left, vertically, horizontally, or diagonally.

Blue Moon

East of the Sun

Full Moon

Moonglow

Moonlight Bay

Rain

Silvermoon

Skylark

Stardust

Sundown

```
S  A  Z  X  M  Y  P  Q  T  H  E  N  O  O  M  E  U  L  B
T  I  L  A  L  L  B  A  U  S  S  W  Y  A  O  N  L  E  J
A  A  L  V  A  S  E  B  I  F  U  L  L  M  O  O  N  F  N
R  A  B  V  E  C  U  I  B  N  A  H  N  G  N  T  O  P  K
D  Y  D  C  E  S  T  N  E  I  I  B  M  R  L  S  C  D  O
U  E  I  V  D  R  F  C  D  I  K  A  L  Q  I  G  U  H  L
S  E  Q  I  W  E  M  J  D  O  J  I  R  J  G  T  K  L  P
T  F  M  E  N  X  Y  O  O  G  W  P  Q  H  H  R  P  S  M
H  R  W  O  L  G  N  O  O  M  W  N  F  G  T  O  I  I  Q
G  E  S  F  T  U  Z  V  E  N  I  X  D  N  B  Y  Z  A  R
E  A  S  T  O  F  T  H  E  S  U  N  A  K  A  C  L  M  T
J  K  A  G  H  E  N  L  O  M  E  B  S  K  Y  L  A  R  K
```

Figure 27

CHRISTMAS CAROLS

Grades: 2 - 8

Materials: Recordings and/or musical scores to Christmas carols.

Concept:

Christmas carols may be used for ear-training activities.

Activities
&
Directions

Music teachers are often surprised, nowadays, that children no longer know the whole vast array of Christmas songs and carols. Do your pupils know all of those listed below? Can they sing them or whistle them? Or, even better as a challenge, can they listen to an instrumental version that you play for them and "Name That Tune" by giving you the song's title?

The First Noel	Christmas in Killarney
Mistletoe and Holly	Twelve Days of Christmas
We Wish You a Merry Christmas	It's Beginning to Look Like
Silent Night	Christmas
Jingle Bells	Nuttin for Christmas
Santa Baby	Rudolph the Red Nosed Reindeer
Frosty the Snowman	I Saw Mommy Kissing Santa
'Twas the Night Before Christmas	Claus
Christmas Song (Chestnuts	Sleigh Ride
Roasting on an Open Fire)	We Three Kings
I'll Be Home for Christmas	Oh Holy Night
It Came Upon a Midnight Clear	Deck the Halls
God Rest Ye Merry Gentlemen	Silver Bells
(All I Want For Christmas Is)	Joy to the World
My Two Front Teeth	Home for the Holidays
The Christmas Waltz	Let it Snow, Let it Snow,
Happy Holiday	Let it Snow
I Saw Three Ships	Santa Claus Is Coming to Town
Oh Christmas Tree	O Come All Ye Faithful
White Christmas	Do You Hear What I Hear?
Winter Wonderland	We Three Kings of Orient Are

Try this lesson early in the Christmas season, perhaps even in November, and see if you and your students don't both start listening more attentively to titles after carols are played on the radio.

TAP THAT TUNE

Grades: K - 4

Materials: None.

Concept:

Tapping rhythms to songs helps one to listen and think.

Activities
&
Directions

Everyone knows the rhythm of the first movement of Symphony No. 5 in C Minor by Beethoven, and many people have learned that its rhythm in Morse code (short-short-short-long, or di-di-di-da ••• —) is the sound for the letter "V" and has been implied to mean victory. But what about the rhythm being similar for the opening of "The Star-Spangled Banner" and "Happy Birthday" (short-short-long-long-long-longer, or (•• — — — —)? Playing a game of "Tap That Tune" can be a lot of fun because many songs have the same rhythm. Children will argue: "That's Yankee Doodle," or, "That's not Yankee Doodle, it's Twinkle Twinkle Little Star," for a good five minutes after they hear the rhythm tapped. (It happens to be the same for both!) It is six short and one long (•••••• —), if you used the words "Yankee Doodle went to town."

"Tap That Tune" is played quite easily. The one who is *it* taps out a tune on the desk or a table, or simply claps her hands. The rest of the class tries to guess what song she has in mind. The easiest song to do is "Jingle Bells"—short-short-long, short-short-long (•• — •• —). In fact, if you cannot get anyone to be *it* in short order, draw Figure 28 on the chalkboard.

RHYTHM GAME

Short   Short   Long,   Short   Short   Long
•   •   —   •   •   —

Name   this   tune,   what   song's   this ?

(<u>See</u>   <u>if</u>   <u>your</u>   <u>pupils</u>   <u>will</u>   <u>answer</u>)

Jin–gle   Bells,   Jin–gle   Bells

Figure 28

MUSIC MAKES YOU. . .

Grades: K - 8

Concept:

Some songs suggest and motivate movement.

Activities
&
Directions

Unfortunately, all good things must come to an end. So, in closing this chapter, we felt that we might as well emphasize the positive "suggestive" role of certain tunes or melodies. On the chalkboard, write the following:

Q. NAME THAT TUNE which makes you smile.
A. "When You're Smiling" or "Smile."

Have your students make a chart such as the one below. Their answers might be totally different, and variety is the spice of life. If they list songs you never heard of, you will listen to them—won't you?

NAME THAT TUNE Which Makes You	Possible Answers
laugh	— Itsy Bitsy, Teenie Weenie, Yellow Polka Dot Bikini
clap hands	— He's Got the Whole World In His Hands
get in a circle	— Hokey Pokey
	— Hava Nagila
feel "togetherness"	— Hail, Hail, the Gang's All Here
march around	— When the Saints Go Marching In
move your hands in gesture or charade	— My Hat It Has Three Corners
	— Alouette
join arms and sway from side to side	— East Side West Side
swing your arms (as with a bat in hands)	— Take Me Out to the Ballgame
jump up and down	— Mexican Hat Dance
fall down	— London Bridge Is Falling Down
skip	— The Farmer in the Dell
	— Skip, Skip Skip to My Lou

9

Enjoying Listening for a Change

To children, fun is frolic—fable—fantastic—foolish—and fast; fun is not being bored. Rossini said that there was no such thing as good and bad music; only good music and the boring kind! Well! Countless generations of children grew up thinking that any music called "classical" had to be dull. Anything that was too popular, or too lively, was immediately designated as "light classical" and a program of "light classical" music became known as a "pops concert." Anyone who has seen Arthur Fiedler and his Boston Pops concerts knows that everyone appears to be having fun! So what's wrong with that?

"Classical music" that is sufficiently profound or sophisticated is sometimes called "serious," the implication being that music which aims for commercial success and immediate consumption is not "serious." Actually, it is a romantic notion that most good music was a failure in its own time. With several notable exceptions, most of the composers we know as "classical" were the popular composers of their age. "Classical" refers to something that has withstood the test of time; posterity decides whether music has lasting value. Music that is fun now just might also be fun tomorrow!

If we can make any sort of a lasting contribution to music education in this chapter, it is to upset the notion that in order to be called "classical," music first has to be sufficiently profound, complex, and uninteresting! One only has to peruse the literature to observe that there is much that is light-hearted in classical music. From Donizetti's *Daughter of the Regiment* to Gilbert and Sullivan operettas, fun and frolic abound in the so-called "se-

147

rious" domain. Even Wagner's opera, *Die Meistersinger*, has its lighter moments.

Some beginning books on music try to teach concepts so advanced that even graduate students in musicology don't understand them fully. The idea of "Enjoying Listening for a Change" merely means applying Rossini's idea of using music that is exciting rather than pieces that we have been told are "good." Let's not be too quick to judge. Start with music of all types that is enjoyable to children—and have fun!

THE KNOWN TO THE UNKNOWN

Grades: 1 - 8

Materials: Rossini's *William Tell* Overture; Tchaikovsky's *1812* Overture; Recordings of Bach and Handel.

Concept:

Contemporary music has its roots in the past.

**Activities
&
Directions**

"From the known to the unknown" has been an acceptable adage in education for quite some time. Unfortunately, it is too often disregarded! What this means in music education is starting with a familiar recording, extracting or analyzing its roots, and building a perceptual basis for knowledge. If children know the *William Tell* Overture through the "Lone Ranger" (are we dating ourselves?), or the *1812* Overture through a breakfast cereal commercial, you can start with what they know. If they smile when you play it, you have "a foot in the door."

Another aspect of teacher preparation is to listen to the popular radio stations (both AM and FM) for recordings that can be used to illustrate how an arranger has used a historical technique. Purchase the record or cassette tape. Together with your pupils, play the contemporary recording that has its roots in the past. Stop at the point where the "ancient sounds" are. Tell the children that you intend to search for "original" recordings using that sound—that is, music composed many years ago. If you, yourself, do your "homework," at a later date you can come back to the students with a recording of the music of Bach or Handel, or whatever style was imitated on the popular recording. Try to get students to compare the two recordings, without you, yourself, doing too much talking.

18 WAYS TO MAKE YOUR PUPILS WANT TO COME TO THE MUSIC CLASS

There are at least eighteen ways to make your pupils want to come to the music class to enjoy listening:

1. Start with music they enjoy listening to anyway—music they listen to at parties or gathered around a juke box;

2. Let your students dance to popular music—an activity they already enjoy and have fun with; but, as soon as possible, shift the focus from dancing to listening by changing the tempo (speed), volume (loudness), and beat;

3. Make a pre-recorded tape in which you mix very short excerpts of waltzes, tangos, rhumbas, boleros, lindies (and other dances which used to be popular) along with current pop music; disregard students' reactions to interruptions of the recordings they prefer;

4. Establish a procedure in which students are permitted to talk while the music is on, before you insist upon "quiet-attentive" listening; this will help to associate music with relaxation and fun—music will soon become a vehicle for enjoyment rather than work;

5. Encourage your pupils to draw to music—structuring topics that relate to musical concepts of largeness, smallness, loudness, softness, fastness, slowness;

6. Let your students read or do homework while listening to music; many children interviewed for this book told us that music helps them relax and concentrate—and "it's more fun to do homework while music is on";

7. Foster movement while listening, but focus on listening in the sense of free movement (beginning choreography) that follows the music; teach movement in rondo form, for example (a b,   a c,   a b,   a); the focus here is not on creative movement but on movement following the music to reinforce recognition; in the lower grades, you may also use a rhythm band wherein children try to imitate instruments they hear;

8. When you introduce classical music, start with music that uses nursery tunes and other well-known melodies; utilize pieces especially written for children and "light classics." Music teachers have found these to be pieces which children respond to favorably;

9. Play "Name That Tune" frequently to create an environment of fun and games, and to avoid any unpleasantness being associated with

music (see Chapter 8); use current popular music, commercials, and television theme music to increase the chances of getting correct answers;

10. Use music that tells a story—"program music"; be sure to select stories that are interesting to children such as *Tam O'Shanter, Til Eulenspiegel,* and *Peer Gynt,* or stories that evoke laughter, such as *The Sorceror's Apprentice;* you might want to read many stories to your class first, giving your pupils a choice of which pieces of music they want to hear (participation in the selection process enhances pleasure);

11. Use small words, clear explanations, and clear illustrations of the concepts you want to teach; your students will find it easier to listen and absorb what you're saying;

12. Let students try their hand at composing by starting with very slight modifications of known melodies or lyrics; creativity should be encouraged as much as possible;

13. Always include some seasonal or occasion music (see Adler & McCarroll, *Elementary Teacher's Music Almanack,* Parker, 1978) so that students are always surprised with something (a composer's birthday, a state holiday, an ethnic celebration, etc.);

14. With younger students, have parades and costume parties when the occasion, holiday, or music warrants it (such as Halloween, Chinese New Year, St. Patrick's Day);

15. Have students conduct music they listen to as often as possible— especially if the music has a distinct profile such as Beethoven's Fifth Symphony or Wagner's *The Ride of the Walküres;*

16. In the upper grades, introduce your pupils to major works, but start with ones that contain humor, such as Mozart's opera, *The Magic Flute;*

17. Explore concepts of "turn-ons" and "turn-offs" with your pupils; be research oriented—what is it they like and why?

18. Incorporate as much contemporary music of all types (including the styles known as "chance music" and electronic music).

MUSIC IS DIVERSITY

Grades: 4 - 8

Materials: Music and music education texts that discuss the many types of music and musical forms.

Concept:

Music can be organized into "its world" and "its power."

**Activities
&
Directions**

Another one of our concerns in this chapter is avoiding the dull aspect of stationary, motionless listening to music. One way to do this is to describe the "World and Power" of music, rather than using less interesting ways of listing compositions. Music is so diverse and filled with emotional experience. Why not draw upon the vitality of such grouping? As you read these next paragraphs, you might start thinking of specific recordings or tapes to use in your classroom (making lists of these recordings according to the categories we describe).

Explain to your pupils that the "world of music" has many aspects. It consists of many forms and activities. Among them are:

opera
symphony
ballet and dance
chamber music
jazz and popular styles
religious music
Broadway and the theater
ethnic music
radio, television, and the movies
muzak
vocal recitals
band concerts

Explain to your pupils that there is also what we call the "power of music." It too consists of many forms and activities. Among its uses are:

for relaxation
in schools
on the football field
to herald victory and celebrate triumph
in prayer
in music therapy
to create suspense
to depict love

to paint mental pictures of fields, streams, oceans
to bring people together

Such is the "power of music" in literature, art, and in our lives. Can you begin to think of music, with which you are familiar, that you can use to illustrate the "world and power" of music? Can you begin to make lists of recordings and tapes you might use? At any rate, considering the diversity of the "world and power" of music, don't make Music Appreciation a "turn-off" by limiting the styles and activities with which you deal.

TURN-OFFS AND TURN-ONS

Grades: 2 - 8

Materials: Music of the Renaissance; harpsichord music; tape recorder and tapes; pop tunes with classical sounds; any opera recordings or rock operas such as *Tommy* or *Jesus Christ Superstar.*

Concept:

Students can be "turned on" to music with positive approaches.

Activities
&
Directions

Let's examine and compare "turn-offs" in music with "turn-ons." Which answers would you have given prior to reading this chapter?

Turn-Off To Television

Student Question:

Did you watch X on television last night?

Teacher Answer:

*I don't watch that junk. We only deal
with good music here.*

Unfortunately, it is still not obvious to many music teachers and teachers in general, that peer pressure is very strong. Rejecting completely what the student likes is poor psychology. Consider instead a "turn-on."

Turn-On To Television

Student Question:

Did you watch X on television last night?

Teacher Answer:

*No, I didn't. When is it on? I'll watch it
next week. In fact, if I can tape it, shall I
play it for the class?*

It should be obvious, nowadays, that accepting what students already like fosters a closer relationship of the teacher and student.

Turn-Off to Music Appreciation

Teacher:

*We are going to learn about the history
of music. We will start with the
Medieval and the Renaissance periods.
The dates of the Renaissance . . .*

We learn best when proceeding from the known to the unknown. We also learn best when there is an aesthetic attraction; when we use music that is already in a well-liked style. Verbal explanations can come after a comparison of actual music itself. Consider instead a "turn-on."

Turn-On to Music Appreciation

Teacher:

*I am going to play a contemporary pop
tune (using one that has some basis in
the music of antiquity—something
using a harpsichord, perhaps, or
another old instrument). Raise your
hand when an instrument comes in
whose name you don't know.*

Turn-Off To Opera

*The teacher plays a recording of any opera in
a foreign language on poor equipment,
without telling its story to the pupils.*

The combination of poor fidelity, a language they don't understand, and a style they are not used to, is a guaranteed "turn-off." Consider instead three "turn-ons."

Turn-On #1

The teacher plays a recording of a "rock opera" such as Tommy *or* Jesus Christ Superstar—*something "operatic" that is in English and familiar.*

Turn-On #2

The teacher arranges for a live performance to be given at the school of a Broadway musical gradually building a basis for accepting the operatic style of singing, by combining operatic singing with relevant or contemporary subject matter.

Turn-On #3

The teacher takes a class to a live performance of a children's opera such as Hansel and Gretel, *or a short, comic opera in English—utilizing the added dimensions of scenery and stage to help overcome prejudices in taste.*

TWENTIETH-CENTURY LISTENING MINIATURES

Grades: 1 - 8

Materials: Recordings of the "Top 40" records; samples of flamenco and classical guitar playing; contemporary soul; older "black music" such as blues, gospel, jubilee and spirituals; popular recordings using electronic effects and classical electronic music using synthesizers; pop records using non-Western influences and/or the sitar, koto and balalaika; country and western styles; different types of jazz such as ragtime, dixieland, swing, bebop or progressive jazz; Igor Stravinsky's *Ebony* Concerto; the *Nonesuch Guide to Electronic Music*; albums of television music for "Star Trek" or "Six Million Dollar Man" and movies such as *Planet of the Apes, Star Wars, Battleship Galactica* or *Close Encounters*; music of John Cage; recorded jazz by Olatunji, Herbie Mann or Mongo Santamaria; music of the Caribbean and Africa; Haitian Music; the album *Afro-Jazz Classic* by Hubert Lawes; *Afro-American* Symphony by William Grant Still; the Congolese Mass *Missa Luba*; Brazilian music including bossa novas.

Concept:

Pupils can learn about major twentieth-century influences while starting with contemporary popular music.

Activities
     &
Directions

ROCK, POP, AND SOUL

In 1966, a leading educator suggested that popular music may provide a bridge which the students can cross from the familiar to the unfamiliar. There can be no better approach to enjoying listening for a change! In 1967, the Tanglewood Symposium called for inclusion in the curriculum of more "music of our time," including current, popular music. In 1969, the entire November issue of the *Music Educators Journal* was devoted to rock. Throughout the 1970's, music publishers advertised numerous learning packets that structured popular music for learning musical concepts. So, please cast aside your reservations about using current "top 40" recordings in the classroom, lest you think that you can't teach appreciation of "good" music if you "let that stuff in." You might seize upon the widespread use of guitars in popular music as a point of departure for introducing Flamenco or classical guitar playing. You might start with soul music and then explore other types of black music such as blues, gospel, jubilee, and spirituals. You might proceed from amplification and electronic effects in popular recordings to complete albums that present the Moog synthesizer and electronic music. Finally, you and your students can look for the many pop compositions based on the classics such as a "Fifth of Beethoven" or "Could It Be Magic" and the many compositions using non-Western influences of the sitar, koto, or balalaika. Don't forget that discussing the history of rock 'n' roll (from rhythm and blues to the "new wave" and "punk rock") is of tremendous interest to your pupils—as are pop styles that include Country and Western flavor.

JAZZ

Not that long ago, one expert suggested that modern jazz is a kind of music that lends itself to serious study, and yet, its popular nature tends to speak to the young at heart. Along with pop, jazz would seem to be another bridge to the complexity of "classical" music. On the chalkboard, list the main styles of jazz, such as:

Ragtime
Dixieland
Swing
Bop or Be-bop
Progressive Jazz

When asked, many students will bring in recordings that their parents listen to. Don't be incensed if some pupil blurts out, "My father listens to that junk," as you're trying to illustrate a style! Laugh with your students and then build upon the experience.

We have found that another interesting activity is to use a portable radio to try to find a jazz station. If you do hit upon one, at least some of your children are sure to remark that sometimes a parent puts on such a recording. If sufficient interest is generated, obtain the necessary books to be able to outline the history of jazz (such as the Pantheon book by Martin Williams entitled, *Where's the Melody?*) and discuss the fusion of African and Creole French music that led to jazz. A trend upon which you can capitalize is the reawakening (in the late 1970's) of an interest in ragtime, via the recordings of Eubie Blake and the Scott Joplin rags used in the movie *The Sting* (a movie that is periodically revived in theatres and on television).

To illustrate swing, it is fun to try to get the Duke Ellington tune, "It Don't Mean A Thing If It Ain't Got That Swing." You'll also find that Dixieland recordings are abundant. Commemorative issues of progressive jazz have recently been issued to honor Stan Kenton. Your students can have fun with bop recordings by Dizzy Gillespie and Charlie Parker. They can wear berets and dark glasses as did the original be-boppers). We have found, also, that there has been a renewed interest in the music of the big bands; that recordings of Glen Miller or Tommy Dorsey are known by students and students know how to do the "Lindy"!

After some experience with ragtime, Dixieland, swing, and bop, you might want to take a chance and share with your class how a twentieth century "serious composer," Igor Stravinsky, used a jazz clarinet sound in his *Ebony* Concerto. You can tell your class that Stravinsky wrote the composition for the famous jazz clarinetist and "big band" leader, Woody Herman.

TAPE, SYNTHESIZERS, AND COMPUTERS

When asked about ways in which twentieth century music differs from that of previous eras, many of the students that we interviewed for this book cited amplification, electronics, or tape. (Of course, lower graders may not use sophisticated terminology; but with a little patient questioning they will come up with similar answers in their terms such as "it is louder" and "we have funny noises." You can use such a discussion to introduce your students to electronics. Ask students to bring in all sorts of recordings that use funny, electronic noises. There are plenty!

Soon you can listen together. The *Nonesuch Guide to Electronic Music*, a two-record album, is an excellent resource. Ask your pupils to remember the different sounds of sinus waves, square waves, saw-tooth waves and white noise, for example. Have them raise their hands at particular times for specific noises or sounds; for example, "Raise your hands when you hear white noise." You might be able to get the class's science teacher to discuss a concept such as comparing white noise and white light.

Another activity is to have a "psychedelic" experience by showing colored slides and/or using a device that will combine colored lights to create white light. Regular classroom lights can be turned on and off rapidly to create the effect of a stroboscope or disco light. Students can contribute by bringing in recordings that use electronic effects, such as movie scores for *Planet of the Apes, Star Wars, Battleship Galactica* or *Close Encounters,* or television scores for "Star Trek" or "Six Million Dollar Man."

Have fun illustrating how the invention of musical tape recordings changed the course of modern music in the following way. Take four of your students' favorite recordings and randomly tape four different parts of each record; play the result forwards and backwards; speed up the tape by playing a 3¾ tape at 7½. Discuss how groups like the Beatles and the Rolling Stones speeded up tape to create interesting effects.

Finally, ask your students if they know anything about computer music. You might explain that an analog computer can create a magnetic tape! Some students know about the giant German computers that have been creating some of the background tracks for leading American pop vocalists. Ask them to contribute albums which give credit to "The Munich Machine" and other German computer centers of the music industry.

CHANCE AND ALEATORIC MUSIC

It has been suggested that beginning musical problems must be simple enough to permit children to direct whatever musical understanding they possess toward an immediate solution with a reasonable hope of success. How do you do that with chance and aleatoric music? Well for one thing, you can explain that music of pure chance means that one has absolutely no idea of what is going to happen. John Cage, the man almost totally responsible for this concept, used the Chinese *I Ching* manual of chance to decontrol the composer's or a performer's influence on a piece of music. Even improvisation was not allowed!

Most of John Cage's compositions cannot be duplicated without losing their "chance" meaning, or they would be "frozen chance." But, one "composition" can be reenacted with a great deal of fun. The composition, *Imaginary Landscape* was scored for twelve radios which are manipulated by twenty-four performers. The performers are instructed to play with the dials—not only to get pieces of programs, commercials, and even static, but also to vary the volume at random. Wait until you see the smiles on your children's faces when you tell them that this will be their introduction to chance music!

In 1958, Pierre Boulez, who shortly after became the conductor of the New York Philharmonic Orchestra, wrote an article which appeared in the German magazine *Darmstadter Beitrage* (that's a tongue-twister that you and your class can have fun trying to pronounce). In an article he called "Alea," Boulez criticized many of the things Cage had been doing, such as rolling dice to determine the notes of music to be used in a work. *Alea* means dice in Latin, and the French word *aléatoire* means chancy or risky. At any rate, the terms "chance music" and "aleatoric music" should not be used interchangeably, although they are now. Perhaps you and your older students can discuss this controversy. Cage was structuring music based on pure chance long before the term "aleatoric" came into widespread use as a result of Boulez's now famous article.

Don't forget to add all these new words to your musical vocabulary, and, as you will see in Chapter 11, you can have spelling bees with them. Final fun: take bells at random and have some sort of a lottery to determine the order in which they will be played. You will then be making up your own composition based on chance—and your class can argue whether to call it chance music or aleatoric music!

AFRICAN AND NON-WESTERN MUSIC

How do you go from the known to the unknown with African and non-Western music? How do you go from the simple to the complex? You might start by listing popular recordings that have been influenced by African music. Don't omit Caribbean reflections (Haitian, Afro-Cuban) of African influences. Our research netted recordings that demonstrated parental assistance with the homework assigned: jazz of Olatunji, Herbie Mann, and Mongo Santamaria. The best readers gleaned information from album covers and knew that Herbie Mann played assorted flutes from Africa and South America. Others know about the flutist Hubert Lawes' *Afro-Jazz Classic*. Still others added the names of Yusef Lateef and Ahmed Jamal.

You might also discuss black and/or Moorish influences on the music of Spain. Flamenco music provides another keyhole glimpse of the historical influences of African music. Music of Brazil—especially from Bahia—is another stepping stone to music of the African continent itself. If there is sufficient interest, close your set of listening experiences with any authentic African music you can obtain, carefully noting whether the music is from North Africa, East, West, or South. Use William Grant Still's *Afro-American* Symphony, or the Congolese Mass *Missa Luba*, as bonus material for a class that expresses enough interest in this topic. You can also sing, "Everybody Loves Saturday Night."

If you are lucky enough to obtain a copy of the *Missa Luba* recording, write Figure 29 on the chalkboard. Your students can tap it or snap it if you explain it using Morse code: short-long-short - long-long. This rhythm is that of the African Gourd (a type of maraca).

SYNCOPATED   RHYTHM

S   L   S   L   L

Figure 29

In the course of our research, a sixth grade class designated as "intellectually gifted" produced the following chart:

**Singing Groups, Performers, and Popular Recordings
of the 1960's Which Used Indian Instruments**

Group	Performer	Record	Instrument
The Beatles	George Harrison	*Rubber Soul*	Sitar
The Rolling Stones	Brian Jones	*Paint it Black*	Sitar
The Lemon Pipers		*Green Tambourine and Jelly Jungle*	Sitar and Tabla
The Box Tops	Vincent Bell	*Cry Like a Baby*	Electric Sitar
The Rascals		*Once Upon A Dream and Sattva*	Sitar, Tabla, and Tambour

The students reported that details about the sitar and Indian musicians such as Ravi Shankar were available to them on record jackets. They also reported that some record jackets described the sitar's shape, tonal quality, number of strings, and difficulty in being appreciated by some Westerners because of its sounding off-key or off-pitch to them.

How would your students fare with such an assignment? Maybe not as badly as you think! Be positive! Try it!

10

More Enjoying Listening for a Change

After using popular music as a bridge to the past, proceeding from the more familiar to the less familiar, from the known to the unknown, we may be ready to plunge headlong into the classics. After all, a curriculum that does not expand, introduce, refine, broaden, expose, and analyze, is nothing more than the home or street with a teacher merely sitting in another seat. Interest in current music should not be disregarded; it should be seized upon as a stepping stone—to generate interest in music of the recent past, and to generate interest in musical concepts. But the teacher should also expand horizons, and should introduce music that has a very distant relationship to the music that children hear on the top-ten or top-forty radio stations. In this chapter, the idea is to have fun doing it.

MUSIC TELLS A STORY

Grades: 1 - 6

Concept:

Music that tells a story is called "program music."

**Activities
&
Directions**

One of the types of music which children have always found most interesting is program music, which tells a story. Prokofiev's *Peter and the*

Wolf, Ravel's *Mother Goose,* Mussorgsky's *Pictures at an Exhibition,* and Saint-Saëns' *Dance Macabre* are among the all-time favorites. But there are many more. We suggest the following long-range approach. In addition to using the program music we help you present to your students;

1. Read sections of music appreciation books on program music;

2. Obtain as many of the recordings suggested as you can;

3. From the books read and the record jacket blurbs, learn the stories of the pieces recommended as worthwhile program music;

4. Decide whether you will read the story "as is" or edit it slightly so that it is in your own words;

5. Rewrite some stories and make them into scripts to be distributed; have students make scripts themselves, also, after reading some of the stories;

6. First listen to the music about which sufficient curiosity is aroused; other pieces can come later; build up to something like Richard Strauss's *Till Eulenspiegel* or *Don Quixote.*

THE SORCERER'S APPRENTICE

Grades: K - 5

Materials: A recording of *The Sorcerer's Apprentice* by Paul Dukas; a children's story book about the story, if possible.

Concepts:

1. Sorcerers are associated with magic.
2. Program music tells a story.

Activities
&
Directions

1. Before playing *The Sorcerer's Apprentice,* explain the story in which the apprentice is able to *start* some of the sorcerer's tricks but is unable to make them *stop.* When the sorcerer comes back, he finds brooms flying about with the entire basement flooded with water. Now play the recording, asking your students such questions as,

   Does the music really describe the story?

   Does the music sound mysterious at all, or make them think of Halloween? (Sorcerers are associated with magic, and many music teachers play this piece for Halloween.)

2. It is also fun to point out that Paul Dukas was born in October (October 1), the Halloween month. For a tie-in with social studies, ask your students if they know what the year of Dukas' birth, 1865, was famous for (answer: the end of the Civil War).

GREENSLEEVES IN THE KITCHEN

Grades: K - 4

Materials: Recordings of "Greensleeves" (several different if possible); recording of Ralph Vaughan-Williams' *Fantasia on Greensleeves*; sheet music or a book of music containing the song "Greensleeves" and/or "What Child is This?"; also, "Overture" and "March Past of the Kitchen Utensils" from the suite made from the incidental music to *The Wasps*.

Concepts:

1. Many composers use folk songs in their compositions—such as the old English song "Greensleeves"; this is sometimes called "nationalism" in music.

2. Some musical stories can be funny.

Activities
&
Directions

1. It is fun to call for some immediate associations with "merry old England"—London Bridge, Winchester Cathedral, the Tower of London, Buckingham Palace, or the white cliffs of Dover. For added enjoyment you might have your students say: "Hip, Hip, Hooray!" and all that "stiff upper lip, old boy," etc. Show a map of the British Isles, and have children point to the famous English Channel that people try to swim. This can be real fun and we've enjoyed this type of background activity with pupils.

2. After the background map work, have fun by playing a recording of Greensleeves such as that by The Weavers, and sing along with the record. Now play Vaughan-Williams' *Fantasia* to see what he did with the melody, and how he embellished it. Point out that the use of the song "Greensleeves" somehow makes the music sound English—and thus is "nationalistic."

3. Younger students in the lower grades will find "March Past of the Kitchen Utensils" particularly delightful. Just thinking of kitchen

utensils marching should make them giggle. Children can get up and march around the room, making believe they are knives and forks and spoons. We have had success with this lesson, because the movement enhances listening pleasure.

4. Other teachers have had success with the "Overture" from Ralph Vaughan-Williams' suite, *The Wasps.* You can point out, in this section of *The Wasps,* that the "buzz" at the beginning can sound like a fly, bumblebee, or a wasp. You'll find that, as with "mouth pops" and other noises, younger children like to hum and buzz—and this section of Ralph Vaughan-Williams' composition permits you to structure the noise. They can also fidget—but purposely fidget the way a fly or a bug does.

DESCRIPTIVE MUSIC

Grades: K - 5

Materials: A recording of *Danse Macabre* by Camille Saint-Saëns.

Concepts:

1. Music that paints a picture or tells a story is called "descriptive music," or program music.

2. Sometimes composers write music that is identified with the season in which they were born.

**Activities
&
Directions**

1. It is fun to point out that certain composers wrote a lot of music that can be identified with their birthday (such as *Danse Macabre,* Halloween music, written by Saint-Saëns whose birthday is in October). If this lesson is given near Halloween, encourage students to watch special performances of seasonal programs and pay close attention to the role music plays in creating suspense.

   Before playing the recordings, encourage students to give their impression of what kinds of sounds ghosts might make and also what kinds of activities ghosts might perform when they return to visit us. This lesson can be incorporated into an art lesson in which students draw their impressions of ghosts and cemeteries. They should also be encouraged to act out their feelings.

2. You might find program notes and read them aloud to the class before playing recordings. After hearing music, ask the class if they were able to follow the stories. Play recordings again and tell them what is happening as they listen to the music. (In *Danse Macabre* you hear bones being awakened and dancing about.)

DEBUSSY'S DAUGHTER'S DOLLS

Grades: K - 8

Materials: Recordings of "Golliwog's Cakewalk" from Debussy's *Children's Corner Suite* (obtain both the piano version and the orchestrated version); pictures of an oboe; a doll and/or other toys.

Concepts:

1. Musical description of children's toys.
2. The sound of an oboe.
3. Syncopation, or displacement of a musical accent.

Activities
&
Directions

1. Young children should be interested in the fact that "Golliwog's Cakewalk" is one of several pieces that Debussy wrote to describe his daughter's toys. What a tongue twister to have fun with: "Debussy's daughter's doll"! We've had great success by actually setting up a "children's corner" for students to play in while the music is being played.
2. Call your students' attention to the sound of the oboe, in the orchestrated version of "Golliwog's Cakewalk." You might also try to clap the syncopated rhythms that you hear (see Figure 30). Figure 30 can

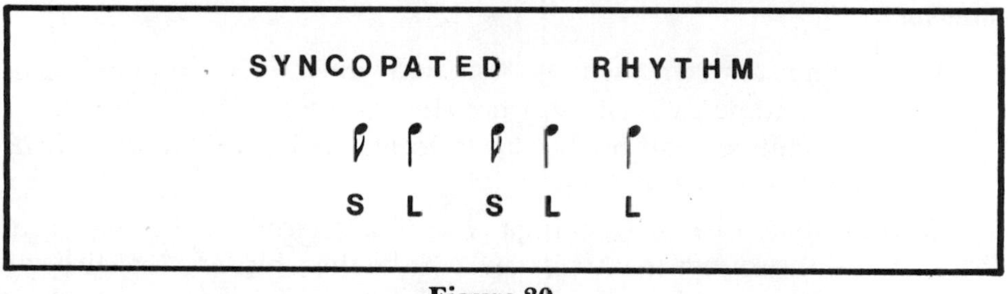

SYNCOPATED   RHYTHM

♪ ♩ ♪ ♩ ♩

S   L   S   L   L

Figure 30

be placed on the chalkboard, and you can have fun trying to guess where it comes in. Does this syncopation look like what it is, a displacement of the beat and a shifting of the regular accent?

3. Older students might discuss the tragedy of Claude Debussy's having been killed in Paris during the World War I aerial bombardment—possibly leading into a discussion of World War I and its causes. Oddly enough, he was killed on the exact same day—March 25—as the day on which another twentieth century master, Bela Bartok, was born. For those students who like to have fun with numbers, the year of Debussy's death was 19*18* and the year of Bartok's birth was 18*81*. Strangely too, there is alliteration in *Bartok's birth* and *Debussy's death*. Bartok's composition *Allegro Barbaro* can be contrasted with "Golliwog's Cakewalk." Whereas the cakewalk uses syncopated, jazz-like rhythms, *Allegro Barbaro* uses rhythms that were considered "barbaric" or "primitive" at the beginning of the century when it was written (1910). Barbarism of primitivism was an early twentieth century style that Igor Stravinsky also used (for example in *The Rite of Spring*).

TRAIN-ED MUSIC

Grades: K - 8

Materials: Swiss cheese; pictures of trains and/or toy trains; recording of *Pacific 231* by Arthur Honegger.

Concepts:

1. Trains can be described musically.
2. Locomotive engines make loud noises.

Activities
&
Directions

1. A good background activity—especially for younger children—can be to eat some Swiss cheese, since Honegger was of Swiss parentage. Older children can use a map to locate Le Havre, France, where Honegger was born.

2. Immediately before listening to *Pacific 231*, children of all ages can recall the sounds that trains make (from the whistle to the clickety-clack on the tracks). Many teachers have found that young children

in particular love to make the "who whoo" sound of the train. While you and your class are listening, try to hear the way the sound of a heavy train is created.

3. Music teachers often point out that Arthur Honegger was a member of a group of French composers called *Les Six*. This group reacted strongly against all trends of the twentieth century: impressionism of Debussy; barbarism of Bartok and Stravinsky; and the dissonance and expressionism of Schoenberg, Berg, and Webern.

DUKE, BESSIE, BILLIE AND ELLA

Grades: 2 - 8

Materials: Any recordings of Bessie Smith, Billie Holiday, Ella Fitzgerald, or the Duke Ellington Orchestra; Duke Ellington's autobiography, *Music is My Mistress*; chalk and chalkboard.

Concepts:

1. Bessie Smith attained nationwide popularity as a singer of the blues.
2. Billie Holiday had a tragic life, eventually dying of a combination of alcoholism and drug addiction.
3. Ella Fitzgerald and Duke Ellington have been listed among the all-time greats in jazz.

Activities
&
Directions

1. There is such a wealth of recordings by Duke Ellington—much of it jazz, but some of it actually classical music. The choice is yours, but if you want to try his classical music, there is the *Black, Beige, and Brown* suite. If you want to stick with the light stuff, why not listen to his version of "April in Paris"? It is one of the best!

2. You may have seen the movie, *Lady Sings the Blues*. Have any of your students seen it? It vividly depicts Billie Holiday's tragic life. You might relate this topic to Bessie Smith singing the blues, and older students can compare definitions of what the blues is. Many of Bessie Smith's recordings are collector's items and hard to find; recordings by Ella Fitzgerald are more plentiful and feature a more modern style of jazz, be-bop and "scat" singing (another great topic for student reports).

FORWARDS AND BACKWARDS: EASY-TO-PLAY MUSIC

Grades: 3 - 8

Materials: Books which describe Hindemith's music and the style of *Gebrauchsmusik* (easy-to-play music); recordings of music considered *Gebrauchsmusik*.

Concept:

Gebrauchsmusik was a term coined by Paul Hindemith to mean easy-to-play, easy-to-understand, "workaday" music. It was an attempt to simplify music that was getting very complex, very dissonant, and often hard to listen to. It was a style fashionable largely in the 1920's and 1930's.

Activities
&
Directions

Your children might find the concept of Hindemith's opera, *Hin und Zuruck*, interesting. The concept is the same as the title, meaning "forwards and backwards." The opera is performed forwards during the first half and backwards for the second half. What fun you and your class will have with this! Can you just imagine them on an auditorium stage, first bringing in something on a tray, later walking backwards with the same tray? Can you imagine all the slapstick routines that can be used? We're sure that you can even update the scenes to make them even funnier. Some teachers have used the basic idea for an original production, and audiences have found it hilarious. Try it!

SOUND ALIKES

Grades: 1 - 8

Materials: Recordings of and/or music for "Happy Birthday to You," our national anthem, the "Star Spangled Banner," Haydn's *Surprise Symphony*, and Mozart's "Ah, vous dirai je maman" ("Twinkle Twinkle Little Star").

Concepts:

1. Some pieces of music have the same rhythm but different melodic directions.
2. The funny term "tune-sleuth" is used for a musicologist who compares melodies.

**Activities
&
Directions**

1. Once upon a time there were writers on music who got to be known as "tune-sleuths." They were very good at demonstrating that one tune or melody was very similar to another. Often, they demonstrated that a popular tune was, indeed, amazingly similar to one in a classical composition. You can see that not everyone would like such people—especially the composers who were guilty of plagiarism (knowingly or unknowingly). Even "university types" looked down upon this activity as not worthy of a musicologist (believing that there were other more important things to do). Ask your students what they think. What if they were a popular composer who was guilty of borrowing a melody from a classical composition? You might improvise a short skit, based on this idea, perhaps one in which a popular composer is confronted by a "tune-sleuth" as having stolen a melody without identifying his source.

2. Now that we are in an age of eclecticism, perhaps we can afford the luxury of such silliness again. A case in point is the similarity of "Twinkle Twinkle Little Star" and the tune from Haydn's *Surprise* Symphony that sounds almost like it. Have your pupils listen to both and compare the differences and similarities. Listen also to Mozart's "Ah, vous dirai je maman" in which he composed many variations on this French tune that we have come to know as "Twinkle Twinkle Little Star." Another example of different melodies that have almost identical rhythms is the similarity of our national anthem, "The Star-Spangled Banner" and the much sung "Happy Birthday to You." While singing the songs very, very softly to yourself, clap the melodies in order to see how the rhythms are almost identical. Have your students do the same for them to perceive how very much alike the rhythms are. Did they ever notice this?

THIS IS THE SYMPHONY THAT SCHUBERT WROTE BUT NEVER FINISHED

Grades: 3 - 8

Materials: Schubert's *Unfinished* Symphony.

Concept:

Words can be used to help remember a melody.

Activities
&
Directions

For many years it was fashionable to denigrate music teachers who used catchy phrases to teach "the classics." For years, some people complained that they could not listen to certain symphonies without thinking of those phrases. However, when this type of teaching stopped, many of the new teachers were even less successful at teaching "the classics." The title of this lesson, the words "This is the symphony that Schubert wrote but never finished," was used at one time to help students memorize one melodic theme for Schubert's *Unfinished* Symphony. We don't see anything objectionable to this approach, except that often mere memorization of as many as fifty different melodies was the sole objective. If this approach can be incorporated into lessons that aim for more than that—real enjoyment and creativity—why not use it? Perhaps your students can write their own parodies of famous classical melodies. Creativity can be fostered without forcing anything on pupils that they might consider too corny or trite.

FOLLOW THE SCORE

Grades: 4 - 8

Materials: Graph paper, crayons or colored pencils, John Cage's book, *Notations.*

Concepts:

1. Students can create their own symbols for music.
2. Twentieth-century composers have searched for new ways of notating modern music.

Activities
&
Directions

1. With your class, make a musical score of some original symbols. Choose symbols that you and your class find interesting; and try to depict a piece of music that you know well. You might want to use dots and dashes for fast and slow; you can use darker colors for louder music and lighter colors for softer music; you might even use graph paper to be able to indicate high and low sounds. Try to avoid thinking that anything you do is wrong. You might be trying to rediscover the wheel, but anything you do to try to reenact the way people first started to try to notate music is acceptable.

2. If you can locate a copy of John Cage's *Notations,* you and your pupils can have a lot of fun seeing how many modern composers searched for new ways of notating music—music that can no longer be notated in traditional ways for one reason or another. You might also examine how music was written very long ago. (Try to "follow the score" if you locate examples of old music notation. Try to imagine what it sounds like and then obtain a recording of music from that period. Does it sound the way it looks?

MULTI-MEDIA

Grades: K - 6

Materials: Films and filmstrips of concerts and operas.

Concept:

Children's listening habits are different from those of adults.

Activities
&
Directions

Your students are fully capable of doing at least two things at once. They might have more fun "enjoying listening for a change" if they were permitted to do what is natural for them, squirm, fidget, play with things in their hands, etc. Why fight it? We have found that too many teachers are always yelling at children to listen when they *are* listening; they just don't look like they are listening!

The more multi-media you use to try to capture their attention, the better chance you will have. Films and filmstrips are fine if they are modern (try to avoid very old films with funny looking clothing and haircuts), in color, and have good fidelity. However, if you do show an old film of an opera or an orchestral concert, when the students laugh be sure to laugh with them or, at least, don't try to suppress the laughter. Trying to suppress their amusement is the worst thing you can do, because you are fighting their instinct to have fun. You want to utilize that "sense of fun."

See if you can "tune in" to the way the latest television programs for children are structured. The "pros" know what sells and what captures children's attention best. Why not pattern yourself after the masters. Try to structure multi-media events (even two films and a television being on simultaneously) so that there is a great deal of excitement and a great deal of visual stimulus.

POINT TO THE INSTRUMENT

Grades: 1 - 6

Materials: Pictures of a full orchestra; pictures of the families of instruments of the orchestra; pictures of individual instruments; recording of Benjamin Britten's *A Young Person's Guide to the Orchestra.*

Concept:

Students hear sounds of instruments almost every day; but many are not acquainted with sounds of many instruments in a symphony orchestra.

Activities
&
Directions

1. First, listen to Benjamin Britten's *A Young Person's Guide to the Orchestra* so you know the order in which instruments will be heard on the recording. Arrange pictures of instruments of the orchestra to correspond with the recording. Then, as you play the recording, hold up or point to a picture of the instrument being described so that students can see what it looks like. You might also write its name on the chalkboard, so that students can see that it is not always spelled exactly as it sounds.

2. Near the end of the Britten recording, where the instruments come in rapidly, but in the order in which they were first heard, have the students point to each instrument when it begins to play. Can they also point to the name of the instrument on the chalkboard?

3. Young children like to hear little songs about choosing or identifying instruments. One we made up is:

    Point to the instrument you want to play,

    The instrument that you want to play today.

    Perhaps you and your students can add lines to it.

4. Older students can learn about the families of instruments:

    Strings

    Woodwinds

    Brass

    Percussion

    If you have enough pictures, they can point to the instruments of the different families. The strings are violins, violas, cellos, and double basses. The woodwinds are flutes, oboes, clarinets, and bassoons. (Music teachers like to explain that the flute used to be made of wood and, therefore, is a member of the woodwind family; and to explain that the clarinet is a single-reed instrument while the oboe and bassoon are double-reed instruments.) The brass are trumpets, trombones, French horns, and tubas. Finally, there are many percussion instruments, but the one that is almost always present is called a kettle drum. Kettle drums in Italian are called timpani or tympani.

A SMALL CONCERTO AND THE LICORICE STICK

Grades: 1 - 7

Materials: Pictures of a clarinet; recordings by Benny Goodman, either jazz or classical; recording of Concertino for Clarinet and Orchestra, Opus 26, by Carl Maria von Weber.

Concepts:

1. Aside from the saxophone, the clarinet is the most recent addition to the woodwind family in the symphony orchestra.

2. The clarinet, a classical or jazz instrument, is known in jazz as a "licorice stick."

3. Benny Goodman was nicknamed the "King of Swing."

**Activities
&
Directions**

1. As background for listening to the Concertino for Clarinet and Orchestra you can show pictures of clarinets, or explain that the clarinet is a reed instrument and a member of the woodwind family. It is fun to point out that the reed used to play the clarinet is made from bamboo cane. You might also explain that the unique sound of the instrument is often best displayed through a concerto (in which the solo instrument is prominent). This is the case with Weber's Concertino; you really get a chance to hear the sound of the clarinet—both in the low register and the high registers, in which the quality of sounds are different.

2. The "funny-sounding" word, "concertino," meaning small concerto, can also be explained. Will your students be able to guess what language "concertino" is, and which syllable means "small"? (Answer: "*ino.*") And why did a German composer use the Italian

language? Some discussion can be had regarding the use of Italian as the "universal language" in music. Be sure your students know that a concerto is a composition for orchestra and a solo instrument, and a concertino is a small composition for orchestra and solo instrument.

3. Benny Goodman has made so many recordings, both of jazz and classical music, that you may have difficulty making a selection. In jazz, Benny Goodman (the "King of Swing") played the "licorice stick" (or the clarinet). You might get some giggles when younger children hear the term "licorice stick" used for the clarinet. But, the funny term, we have found, makes the instrument easy to remember. Funny terms, and "fun lessons," make for life-long interest.

HIGH NOTES ON THE TRUMPET

Grades: K - 6

Materials: Any recordings by Maynard Ferguson.

Concept:

Maynard Ferguson has distinguished himself from other modern jazz trumpet players by specializing in playing in the extreme high register of the trumpet.

**Activities
&
Directions**

Using any Maynard Ferguson recording, listen for the extreme high registers of the trumpet. No other player has consistently played in this register. Others have played faster, better, or with more soul; but higher? Rarely! Some of your younger students might even put their fingers to their ears when they hear the very high notes. But, like spinning and getting dizzy, children sometimes have fun with high, whining, even painful noises. Moreover, once having heard this sound, they will never forget it.

A MUSICAL BARBER

Grades: 2 - 6

Materials: A recording of Samuel Barber's *Adagio for Strings.*

Concepts:

1. A string orchestra has no percussion, brass or woodwind instruments.

2. *Adagio* is an Italian word meaning the music is to be played slowly.

**Activities
&
Directions**

1. No—this musical barber is not *The Barber of Seville*; it is our very own Samuel Barber who was born in West Chester, Pennsylvania. Can your students find it on a map? How far is it from Hershey, Pennsylvania, where you get all that *scrumptious* chocolate? (Pop a few chocolate candies in students' mouths and see some real fun-filled faces!)

2. Samuel Barber's *Adagio for Strings* uses only string instruments. Have your pupils name the missing families of instruments (answer: woodwinds, percussion, and brass). Have them name the instruments of the string family (answer: violins, violas, cellos, and double basses).

3. You might want to ask your students if they have any idea of what *adagio* means, or what language it is. If you've discussed the frequent use of Italian terms in music before, they might correctly guess Italian. And after listening to the composition more than once, especially if you give them a hint that *adagio* has to do with the speed or tempo of the music, they might correctly guess that *adagio* means very slowly or in a leisurely manner.

4. A related creative activity can be to develop the concept of how string instruments make their sounds by vibrating. The easiest way to demonstrate this is by stretching a rubber band and then plucking it, and watching it vibrate.

30 CONDUCTORS

Grades: 3 - 8

Materials: Baton; music stand if available; recordings of Beethoven's Fifth Symphony or Wagner's "Ride of the Walküres."

Concepts:

1. Conductors conduct with a stick called a *baton*. Some conductors do not use a baton.

2. Despite lack of training, students can use gestures similar to those of professional conductors.

**Activities
&
Directions**

1. One of the best ways to get pupils to enjoy music (for a change) is to have them conduct it themselves. We have found that the following lesson is enormously effective. Students stand up around the room— with or without music stands. As a recording is played, students will try to conduct the music. The students who are not conducting will act as an audience that applauds the conductor before he starts conducting, and applauds after the piece is over.

2. Use a composition the students have come to enjoy because of its unique profile (sharply delineated rhythms and accents). We have found Beethoven's Fifth Symphony (first movement) and Wagner's "Ride of the Walküres" to be the best choices—with the *1812* Overture by Tchaikovsky and the "Great Gate of Kiev" by Mussorgsky second best. Of course, you can use any other classical pieces that you and your students find exciting. You might try Smetana's Overture to *The Bartered Bride*, in which there is an exciting polka; or you can try Rossini's Overture to *Il Signor Bruscino*, in which you hear the violinists tapping with the wood of their bows to imitate the sound of a cane knocking on a door.

3. Some students find the history of the baton mildly amusing. It goes back to the fifteenth century when it was the style to beat time for the Sistine Choir in Rome with a roll of paper called a "sol-fa." Perhaps your students can make batons of differing sizes—from nine or ten inches to eighteen in length. Wood can be most easily used; but other materials can be used also. Your "scientific geniuses" can have fun by making a baton that lights up in the dark!

Sounds, Spelling and Movement

In their play, children make noises of sirens, ships' horns, motorcycles, airplanes, brakes screeching, and a car's engine. They also make sounds such as roars, grunts, meows, moos, and barks. Why not capitalize on these natural tendencies and harness this energy in the classroom? Why not utilize this sensitivity to sound to increase perception of how skilled composers use the various different noises in our modern day environment? We have found that children love to make these noises, even in the classroom. Thus, this chapter includes many sounds that young children and adolescents make quite naturally—either imitating something seen in the movies or on television, or through the tradition of children's games that are passed down from generation to generation.

We have also found that students sometimes love to giggle at silly sounds of forced, artificial rhymes. Try making a musical map and ask students to find the tuba in Aruba! Or ask them if they would like some jello on their cello! How about asking them to try to draw a cute flute with a zoot suit? The laughter that you get can be used as a point of departure for learning more about instruments. And if you really want to laugh together, ask younger pupils to spell the names of many common instruments!

These and other ideas are in the chapter to follow, using additional silliness that combines fun with fancy and fantasy. After all, music should be fun, shouldn't it? Then get on the bandwagon and help us make it so.

Figure 31

Grades: 3 - 8

Materials: Chalk and chalkboard or music flashcards.

Concepts:

1. Quarter and half notes.
2. Octaves.
3. The music staff.

Activities
    &
Directions

1. Place Figure 31 on the chalkboard or music flashcards. Have your students copy the figure. Ask them to identify the letter names of the notes (Answers: D, G, and E.) You might also ask your students if they can identify the rhythmic values of D, G, and E. The correct answers are:

   > D — a half note
   >
   > G — an *incorrectly drawn* half note (funny looking?)
   >
   > E — quarter notes

   You might remark that the funny-looking G should have had its stem (the vertical line part of a note) going up on the right side, if it were drawn properly.

2. Another enjoyable way of using Figure 31 is to try to spell words using the letter names of the musical notes. Since the notes are D, G, and two E's, the most obvious word to students, we have found, is E D G E. But, other music teachers have permitted pupils to add the other letters of the musical alphabet (A, B, C, D, E, F, G,) to obtain words such as:

BADGE	FAD
DAB	AGE
FED	EGG

3. If curiosity is aroused by the double notes, this is a perfect opportunity to explain the concept of the *octave*, duplication of a tone eight notes higher (such as C D E F G A B C). (Of course, remind students that there is no H in American music and that A comes after G when going up the scale.)

4. Using Figure 31, students can also come to the board or use music flashcards to spell the words using letters and music. For example,

S	M
O	O
U	V
N	E = quarter notes
D = half note	M
S	E = quarter notes
	N
	T

SIREN

Grades: K - 8

Materials: A recording of *Façade* by Sir William Walton; a siren; pictures of police cars and ambulances.

Concepts:

1. A siren is a sound that gets higher and higher, then gets lower and lower.
2. *Pitch* is the musical term for highness or lowness.
3. It was not until the twentieth century that composers thought of a sound like a siren as a musical sound.

Activities & Directions

1. Children love to imitate a siren with their own vocal chords while

playing games ("cops and robbers" or "hospital"). They merely start way back in their throats with a high pitch and go higher and higher, then back down. This aspect of a natural game can be incorporated into a musical lesson. Children can first hear the word *pitch* and learn its meaning. Or, they can be asked to have a discussion about why composers didn't use sirens in their music until the twentieth century. After all, Verdi used an anvil in his opera *Il Trovatore*, didn't he? The idea of playing a game in class as a prelude to having a musical discussion is one that will set the stage for considering music lessons as being fun rather than being "boring."

2. Another concept that can be explored with this lesson is that of a composer setting poetry to music, or of poetry inspiring music. In *Façade*, Sir William Walton used the poetry of Edith Sitwell, and also used a narrator. Older students can write their own poems about sirens or a parade. Younger students can have poetry read to them.

3. You might want to have a parade with younger children who love movement so much, and who have so much spontaneity when it comes to moving about. Or, using the title of this lesson, you can ask your students if they want to *be* a siren. How does a siren move? How would you feel if you were a siren on top of a police car? How would you feel if you were a siren on an ambulance? Don't forget to post pictures around the room!

SHIP HORN

Grades: K - 8

Materials: Pictures of boats and ships; soda bottles.

Concepts:

1. A foghorn or a ship horn—a "funny sound" to many pupils—has a deep tone that is low in *pitch*.

2. Like a siren, a fog horn moves as the ship goes through the water.

Activities
&
Directions

1. Ships' horns may be hard to come by. But blowing across the top of a soda bottle often produces a sound that sounds almost exactly like a foghorn—especially if you use a large enough bottle or a jug. We have found that younger students like to play being "ships that are

about to collide." In fact, a large part of the fun is banging into each other when they finally do collide. Using the bottles—or the jugs—students who are the ships can make their own foghorn sounds, or other students (from the "audience") can do it.

2. The "funny sound" of a foghorn can be the stimulus that leads to a discussion of why it sounds so funny. Is it because it is so deep a sound, so deep in pitch? This can lead to further discussion, especially with older students, of what makes pitch "high" and "low." You might assign vocabulary words like:

frequency   vibrations

amplitude   sine waves

Do you have any students who can explain why a ship would want to use a low pitch rather than a high one?

BULL HORN

Grades: K - 6

Materials: A bull horn; rolled-up newspapers or magazines.

Concepts:

1. Bull horns are used to amplify the human voice.
2. The forerunner of the bull horn was the megaphone, also having a conical shape but not using batteries.

Activities
&
Directions

1. Many schools use bullhorns for various reasons. They do funny things to the voice and sound funny to children. In fact, we have found that young children who have never heard the term find even the very name "bull horn" to be funny-sounding. Try asking your younger pupils if they have ever heard of a "bull horn." You might be surprised by the number of giggles you get. If you don't have one available to demonstrate, children can cup their hands over their mouths to imitate one. The hands, you can explain, act as an additional resonating chamber. Many teachers have found that this activity is an enjoyable one.

2. Another enjoyable activity is using rolled-up newspapers or magazines to slightly amplify the voice. Of course, you will have to be

careful that the "props" are used in the correct manner. Some of your more capricious pupils might get a bit too frivolous; but we have found that it is worth taking the risk. Why is the voice amplified or made louder? Can any of your students investigate this principle? This can be a very interesting related science activity—especially for older students of the upper grades.

MUSIQUE CONCRÈTE MINIATURES

The concept of *musique concrete* is of sounds that are not generally thought of as music actually becoming part of the musical vocabulary. The concept gradually emerged out of ideas that were revolutionary and experimental from 1907 until the 1950's. But, in recent years, there has been so much use of heretofore nonmusical sounds that the idea has become almost commonplace. Moreover, children take to this concept like ducks to water. They are so used to making different sounds when they play with each other, that when asked to make some of these sounds to be placed on cassette tapes, they respond quite naturally. See if you can expand some of these lesson ideas into a unit of study on understanding modern music and contemporary composers.

Grades: 3 - 8

Materials: Recordings that use the sounds of car engines revving (e.g., Leonard Nimoy's "Hitch-hiker"); motorcycles (e.g., The Shangrilas' "Leader of the Pack"); airplanes (e.g., the Box Tops' "The Letter"); brakes screeching, roars, grunts (e.g., *Batman* or *Bonnie and Clyde*); meows, moos, barks (e.g., The Beatles' "Good Morning" or "Hey Bulldog"; bird calls, the telephone, sea gulls, clinking glass, guns, rain, or thunder.

Concepts:

1. The musical vocabulary is expanding to include new sounds not previously connected with music. Such sounds are called *musique concrète*.
2. *Musique concrete* is a French term coined by Pierre Schaeffer.

MEOWS, MOOS, AND BARKS

**Activities
   &
Directions**

The British rock stars, the Beatles, had many recordings that used sounds of roosters and other farm animals, or dogs—recordings such as

"Good Morning" or "Hey Bulldog." Then there was the distortion of singing which was speeded up as in "The Chipmunk Song." You and your students can provide a more updated list of meows, moos, barks, and other sounds, such as the chart below:

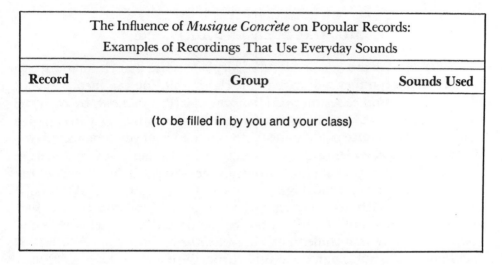

The Influence of *Musique Concrète* on Popular Records: Examples of Recordings That Use Everyday Sounds		
Record	**Group**	**Sounds Used**
(to be filled in by you and your class)		

The preparation of such lists or tables can be fun. While we were doing research on "Pupil Perception of Twentieth Century Music," many students and teachers had a lot of fun along with us. (Moreover, interest in popular records which use nonmusical sounds can be used as a stepping stone toward learning about the futurists or the Italian *bruitissimo* school, the Pierre Schaeffer *musique concrète* school, and John Cage's "prepared piano.")

CAR ENGINE REVVING

Another sound that children will make quite naturally, while playing games, is that of a car engine "revving." Why not incorporate the fun children have playing these games with a lesson on modern music? First, tape the children's imitations of a car engine revving. Have fun playing it back to them and making the volume louder and softer (like a conductor conducting an orchestra). Then, make lists of recordings the pupils can think of which use the sound of an automobile or a racing car (adding in your own older recordings, perhaps, such as Leonard Nimoy's "Hitch-hiker" or Shangrilas' "Leader of the Pack", which used the sounds of motorcycles). You will be surprised at how many recordings your pupils will come up with. Finally, you might go into some music history. We suggest telling your students that early in the twentieth century there was a short-lived Italian "school" of music known as *futurism* or *bruitissimo* (a term sure to get a laugh if you use an Italian accent). A man named Balilla Pratella (an advocate of futurism) called musicians to take account of "the empire of the machine and the power of electricity." He wanted the sounds of motor cars and of airplanes to be added to the repertory of musical sounds. Little did his critics know that fifty years later, world-wide popular music would be doing just that with frequency.

MOTORCYCLE AND AIRPLANE

War movies provide one kind of airplane noise that children love to reenact! What fun they will have in the classroom! You can incorporate it, also, in this lesson series on *musique concrète*. (Pronounced, by the way, "moo-zeek con-cret.") Motorcycle noise is a similar sound, so, you can give your students a choice of the game they want to play. If you tape-record two different students, and then play the results back simultaneously, you will get a weird effect that rivals some electronic music—especially if you distort the sound by taping it at too high a volume. Continuing to make lists of recordings as an activity, you might add *The Letter* by the Box Tops to ones your pupils can think of which use the sound of an airplane. Finally, continue briefing your students on "the *musique concrète* story." Tell them that Pratella's friend Luigi Russolo, also from the Italian "school" of "futurism," issued a "Manifesto of Bruitissimo" in the year 1913. He wrote to Pratella and thoroughly described a "new music of noise." He called for a complete investigation of six types of sounds, including bangs, screams, hisses, whispers, and sobs. This was long before a Frenchman named Pierre Schaeffer and an American named John Cage used these sounds in their musical compositions.

BRAKES SCREECHING

Judging by popular television programs and movies children go to see, the sound of screeching brakes is one that children like. Their young adult heroes often have fun "poppin wheelies" or "burning rubber" (which is zooming off while the brake is still on). The sound of your students imitating screeching brakes can be recorded and added to your classroom repertory of *musique concrète* noises. How about trying some "daffynitions" such as the ones in children's joke books or comic books? Two of the many submitted to us are: (1) *musique concrète* is the sound of unbreakable records; and (2) people walk on concrete and the noise they make is called *musique concrète*. Another activity of course is adding to your list of records using nonmusical sounds—this time trying for ones that use screeching brakes. Finally, you can complete the tale of *musique concrète* (talking in rhyme this time?). Explain that after decades of theory and experimentation, the "futurists" finally got their wish. The inventions of gramophone records and musical tape for tape recordings actually led to a French "school" of music known as *musique concrète*. Its founder and pioneer was a Frenchman named Pierre Schaeffer. In 1947, Schaeffer revived the Italian futurists' attempt to use mechanical and everyday noises in music. Schaeffer used the gramophone to record various everyday sounds as well as musical sounds. Then he manipulated them in different ways to alter them or distort them (a technique that you can learn to do with recorded sounds that your students make). Since the basic tonal material was "real" or *concrète*, he called the result *musique concrète*. Musical tape, as we all know now, not only permits us to record; it also makes it much easier for us to speed up or slow down the sounds we have already recorded, having a lot of fun with distorting sound!

ROARS AND GRUNTS

"Me Tarzan" is a phrase that often precedes a "Tarzan-like" sound that many children make during play. It is a cross between a scream and a roar. Grunts are noises visually portrayed in comic books and in comic strips, and made while playing "Cowboys and Indians" or "Cops and Robbers." Recordings such as *Batman* and *Bonnie and Clyde* had punches and crashing noises in them. Can you and your students list any more? If you want to add to the story of *musique concrète* (and by this time you and your students should have had a lot of fun trying to properly spell all the funny-sounding foreign terms and names), you might tell them about John Cage. In 1949, Pierre Schaeffer met with an American named John Cage. (Pupils with an inclination for laughing at names sometimes find it odd that the word "cage" can also be someone's name!) About this time, Cage was credited with inventing the "prepared piano." The "prepared piano" is a piano in which assorted objects are fitted between the piano strings to make the piano sound completely different. The sound of the prepared piano depends on the objects you put into it. Try it! Actually, folk musicians in America—especially blacks— had done this before him with pianos and banjos; Cage merely formalized the system and made recordings with greater variety. Your students can also, as another activity, create different dances of physical movements for various sounds—along with their natural choreography of "Cowboys and Indians" or "Cops and Robbers."

BIRD CALLS

Immortalized by Walter Lantz, via Woody Woodpecker, the sound of the woodpecker is among the funny sounds in nature. Can any of your

Figure 32

students imitate it? We bet they can imitate the "signature" of Woody Woodpecker* himself (see Figure 32), heard in many cartoons.

Used as a point of departure, this activity can set the stage for a comparison of musical sounds with the sounds of nature. One related activity is to listen to *Chronochromie* by Olivier Messiaen, another composer who went to work at the *musique concrète* laboratory in Paris (be sure to include both the composer's name and the title of the work in any musical spelling bee). In *Chronochromie*, are there real bird calls or are instruments imitating bird calls? You might identify the sounds of bells, the piccolo, the clarinet, and the xylophone, with your students. Can you and your students guess which bird calls are being imitated? Another procedure is to compare the thick, dense sound used to depict the rocks, with the light rippling sounds of the imitation bird calls. Why wasn't a recorded real bird call used—as was the sound of the nightingale in Respighi's *Pines of Rome*? A related activity might be to listen to the jazz of Charlie Parker in a recording of his composition entitled, *Ornithology*. Where are the bird calls? Can you or your students hear any, and how is their distortion different from the way sounds are distorted in *musique concrète*? With older students, this can lead to a discussion of jazz improvisation or variation (two more words for your musical spelling bee). Include "ornithology" as a spelling word too.

FUN AND CARTOON WITH RHYME

As a related activity—or series of activities—you can call upon the artistic and poetic talents of your pupils. Fun with rhyme can help your students learn about as well as how to spell many of the standard instruments. Having fun by rhyming raccoon with bassoon may lead to curiosity about the bassoon—what it looks like, what it sounds like, what family of instruments it is a member of. Having fun by trying to draw "a chimpanzee with timpani" can arouse curiosity about the timpani or kettle drums—its membranes, its mallets, how its pitch changes.

TUBA IN ARUBA

Grades: 2 - 7

Materials: A map of the Caribbean and South America; pictures of brass instruments; crayons and water colors.

Concepts:

1. There are words that rhyme with the names of musical instruments.
2. Nonsense rhymes can become even funnier when made into a cartoon or a comical drawing.

**Activities
&
Directions**

1. Hang up a map of the Caribbean or South America that clearly shows the island of Aruba. Call children up to the map to point to the island country. Ask them to pronounce it, and ask them to name a musical instrument with which it rhymes. Do they know the other instruments of the brass family that the tuba is a part of? (Answer: trumpet, trombone, and French horn.)

2. Given a picture of the tuba, can any of your artistically talented students draw "a tuba in Aruba"? How about "an Aruba tuba"? What's the difference in how a regular tuba looks and the shape of a sousaphone? You might explain that the sousaphone was designed to be carried as part of a marching band, while the regular tuba is played sitting down with a band or orchestra. Encourage the funniest drawings or cartoons that can be made. The funnier the drawings, the more vivid an impression the experience will make. (See Figure 33.)

3. If you are continuing to expand your list of words for a musical spelling bee, you can add:

tuba	Aruba
trombone	sousaphone
French horn	trumpet

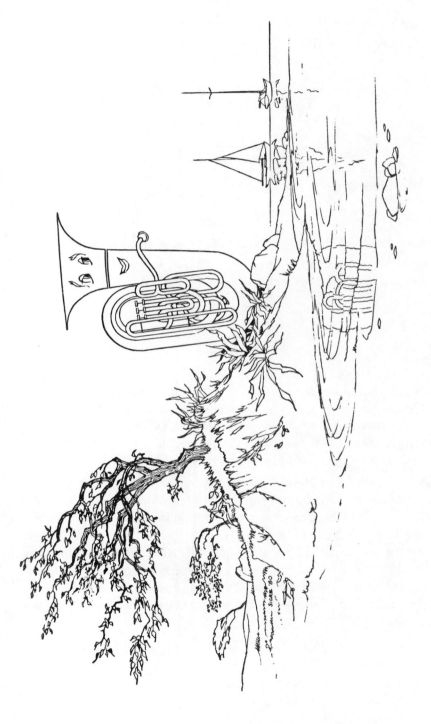

Figure 33

CELLO IN JELLO

Grades: K - 6

Materials: Some gelatin desserts; pictures of the violin, viola, cello, and double bass.

Concepts:

1. The cello is the second largest member of the string family of instruments in an orchestra.
2. Rhyme can be used to help teach proper pronunciation of musical instruments.

Figure 34

Activities
&
Directions

To arouse some initial laughter, ask your pupils if they would like some jello on their cello! Or, ask them if they would like to eat their jello with a cello. The idea is to invite the question, "What's a cello?" Don't forget that if you write "cello" on the chalkboard, your pupils will not automatically supply the necessary "h" to make it sound "chello" as it is properly pronounced. You might explain that a cello is a member of the string family of instruments and is short (an abbreviation of) for violoncello. The other members of the family are the violin, the viola, and the double bass. (Don't forget to add these instruments to your list of words for a musical spelling bee.) Finally, if you show pictures of a cello, can any of your students draw it, either alone or in cartoon form in a bowl of jello? (See Figure 34.)

ICE CREAM CONE IN A TROMBONE

Grades: K - 6

Materials: Pictures of a trombone and trombones mute; a real trombone if it can be obtained; some sugar cones for ice cream and some ice cream.

Concepts:

1. The trombone is a member of the brass family of orchestral instruments.
2. Like other brass instruments, the trombone uses a mute sometimes.
3. A mute is a device placed in the bell of a trombone to soften or muffle the sound.

Activities
&
Directions

Trombones use mutes to soften or muffle the sound. It is very comical, we feel, to see a trombone mute drawn as an ice cream cone. Given the visual stimulus of a picture of a trombone, can any of your artistically talented students rise to the occasion and come up with a sufficiently comical drawing? (See Figure 35.)

Students might also have fun imitating the movement of a trombone player in a jazz band or a marching band. They can also imitate the sound of a

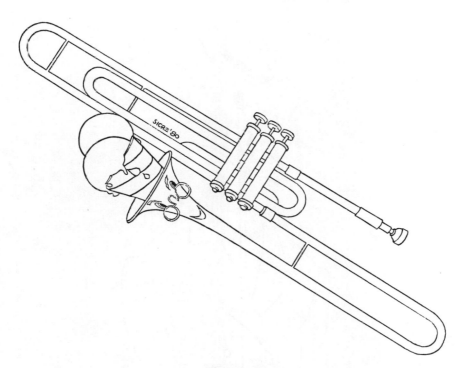

Figure 35

trombone, with or without a mute. Find a recording of Tommy Dorsey and his orchestra, if you can.

FLUTE IN A ZOOT SUIT

Grades: K - 6

Materials: Picures of a flute and other woodwind instruments; pictures of people in zoot suits; oaktag.

Concepts:

    1. Zoot suits were fashionable in the 1940's.

    2. The flute used to be made of wood.

Activities
    &
Directions

    You might have to get an art teacher to come in to try to draw a flute dressed up in a zoot suit! Have your students heard of zoot suits? Do you

Figure 36

remember what zoot suits looked like? Have you seen pictures. Do you have pictures? See if you or a talented student can transfer Figure 36 to the chalkboard or a piece of oaktag. Most students know what a flute sounds like but they may not know that it used to be made of wood—and, therefore, is a member of the woodwind family, along with the clarinet, oboe, and bassoon.

MUSICAL ALPHABET GAME

Grades: 1 - 6

Materials: A piano; a toy piano; a dummy piano keyboard; bells with letters on them such as resonator or Swiss Melode bells.

Concepts:

1. The musical alphabet is A B C D E F G.

2. You can have fun while learning the notes and relationships of the musical alphabet.

**Activities
&
Directions**

1. Have a student observe that the resonator bells clearly indicate which is A, B, C, D, E, F, or G. Ask the student to strike certain bells with a mallet or even a pencil, whose letters spell a word or a name such as A B E. In Figure 37, we have drawn what these notes look like, and you can place the figure on the chalkboard for your pupils.

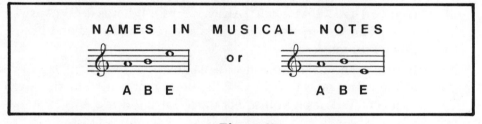

Figure 37

Are there other simple names you can write on a staff using the musical alphabet A B C D E F G ? Can you play them on the bells?

2. The piano can be used once you have explained to your pupils that most pianos start with A, and proceed from left to right with ABC-DEFG, ABCDEFG, ABCDEFG, etc. Swiss Melode bells can be used also, but usually are pitched from F to F (using B flat instead of B natural):

F,G,A,B flat, C, D, E, F,

3. Other words that many music teachers like to use in playing the Musical Alphabet Game are drawn in Figure 38. You can place them on the chalkboard for your students to see.

Unlike advanced musicians, neither you nor your pupils will know what the notes "sound like" beforehand; but, you can have fun trying. Some surprises will be: (1) BAG sounds like "Three Blind

Figure 38

Mice" and (2) DAD sounds like the end of "Are You Sleeping" or "Frère Jacques."

4. Another enjoyable activity is turning music into numbers (and vice versa). If A is 1, B is 2, C is 3, D is 4, E is 5, F is 6, G is 7. D A D would then be 4 1 4. What is cab? (Answer: 3 1 2). What is deaf? (Answer: 4 3 1 6). Can you reverse the process and turn addresses and license plates into music?

5. In turning numbers into music as a game, one who is "it" has to go to the piano or bells and play the notes represented by the given numbers. Will it be a tune? Try the following using A as 1:

5 4 3, 5 4 3	Answer: Three Blind Mice
3 3 3 4 5	Answer: Row, Row, Row Your Boat
3333 5 77 5 3	Answer: Here We Go Round The Mulberry Bush

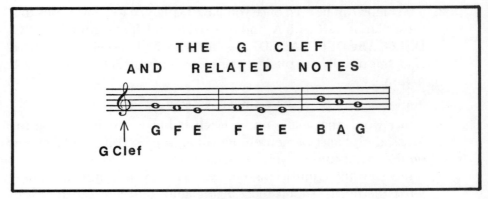

Figure 39

6. You can also teach music reading in game form. Draw five lines as in Figure 39 and add the G clef, explaining that it winds around the second line from the bottom, which is G. Then make a circle wind around the second line and call it G. Explaining that "down" in music is "backwards," show what the words FEE and BAG look like in music.

FINAL FUNNIES: MUSIC AND SPELLING

What instrument rhymes with:

	answer
hobo	oboe
marionette	clarinet
carp	harp

cartoon: carp in a harp?

raccoon	bassoon

cartoon: raccoon with a bassoon?

crumpet	trumpet
thimble	cymbal

Question: Which composers have the word "in" in their names?

Answer: Ross-*in*-i
            Pucc-*in*-i

Question: Which famous opera composer's name can be translated to Joe Green?

Answer: Guiseppi Verdi

12

Mostly Music and Math

In this chapter, you can have fun with counting, giving "treats for beats," learning to add halves through the trumpet and trombone slide and valve positions, learning intervals, having a "rhythm riot," or "playing" on words like "syncopation relation" or "meter à la mode." Children will usually laugh at the big, long word: "semi-hemi-demi-semi-quaver," or the made-up words: "pentapus" or "dodecapus." These are our new "mathematical musi-mals!" And children particularly like the short, Did You Know.

People always relate music and mathematics anyway—so why not have fun with musical and mathematical relationships?

Because so many of these activities came from students, originally, we have had particular fun writing this chapter. We hope you enjoy it as much as we have doing it for you!

FUN WITH COUNTING

Grades: 3 - 7

Materials: Cardboard; Scissors.

**Activities
&
Directions**

Try telling your students the following story: Four people came to dinner, but two of them brought a child, without permission. And, therefore, two of the four large slices of after-dinner pie have to be cut in half. Now, ask them if they are ready for their "mathemusical" or "musimathical," or "musi-matical" questions. Are they? O.K. Here we go!

Question (easy):	How many people in all are there?
Answer:	Six.
Question (still fairly easy):	How many pieces of pie are there in all?
Answer (of course):	Six.
Question (slightly difficult):	How many quarters of the pie are there, and how many eighths?
Answer:	Two quarters and four eighths.
Question (more difficult):	Can you cut out a cardboard circle, cutting the circle into quarters and then cutting two of the quarters into eighths?
Answer (of course):	See Figure 40.

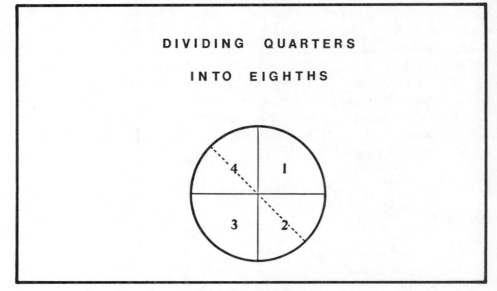

DIVIDING   QUARTERS

INTO   EIGHTS

Figure 40

Question (difficult): Can you draw the musical equivalent of the eighths and quarters of pies?

Answer: See Figure 41.

Q
Ei Ei
Q
Ei Ei
Q
Q
Ei Ei Q
Ei Ei Q
Ei Ei Q

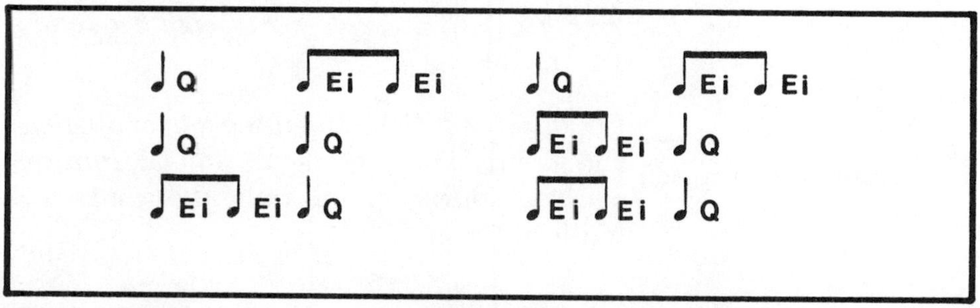

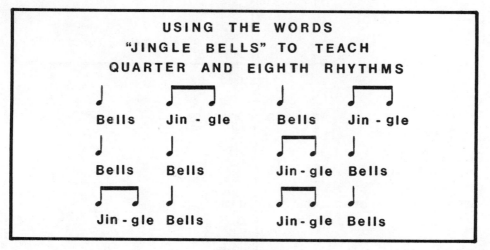

Figure 41

Question (easier again): Using Figure 41, ask your pupils if they know which slice(s) of pie are cut in two according to the musical examples—the first, second, third, or fourth?

Answer: The second and the fourth; then the third; then the first and third.

USING THE WORDS
"JINGLE BELLS" TO TEACH
QUARTER AND EIGHTH RHYTHMS
Bells
Jin - gle
Bells
Jin - gle
Bells
Bells
Jin - gle
Bells
Jin - gle
Bells
Jin - gle
Bells

Figure 42

Question
(much more difficult):   Making the eighth notes go twice as fast as the
quarter notes, can you say *quarter, eighth
eighth, quarter, eighth eighth*? How about *quarter, quarter, eighth eighth quarter*? How about
eighth eighth quarter, eighth eighth quarter?
(See Figure 42.)

Finally: Children always have fun using *tah* for quarters
and *tee* for eighths. Using *tah* and *tee*, can you
and your class clap and recite the words and
music in Figure 43?

Answer:

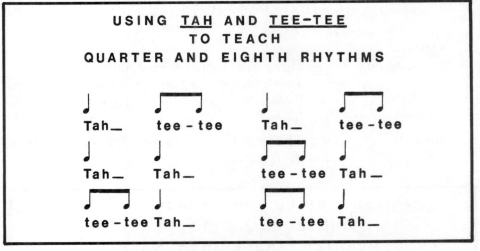

Figure 43

TREATS FOR BEATS

Grades: K - 6

Materials: M&M's, or any other popular candy.

Concept:

Quarter and eighth notes can be learned with different aural, visual
tricks.

Activities
&
Directions

1. Although not inventing the system, B. F. Skinner popularized the system of "operant conditioning" using reward and punishment for behavior modification. Since this chapter is entitled "M & M," we like to use M & M candies as "treats"; but any other candy that children like can be used as a treat or a reward—to make learning beats and rhythms more fun.

2. Place Figure 44A on the chalkboard or on music flashcards. (See lesson entitled "Fun with Counting.") Many music teachers have taught rhythm in different ways. You might add Morse code and "apple pie" to your arsenal of "tricks" to help make rhythms and beats more fun, as in Figure 44B. For example,

Figure 44A

Quarter, Eighth eighth, Quarter, Eighth eighth is now

```
   Slow     fast-fast     Slow     fast-fast
   Pie      Ap-ple        Pie      Ap-ple
   ___        •  •        ___        •  •
```

Figure 44B

When a student gets a beat right, or invents a new "trick" what do you do? Of course, you give him a treat!

TROMBONE AND TRUMPET POSITIONS

Grades: 4 - 8

Materials: Pictures of the trumpet and trombone; actual instruments if available.

Concepts:

1. Learning fractions.
2. Learning Roman numerals.
3. Spelling words through trumpet valve patterns.

**Activities
&
Directions**

1. Place Figures 45 and 46 on the chalkboard. If you have a real trumpet, try to follow the pattern of the fingerings. Point out that the seven trombone positions (usually expressed in Roman numerals) are obtained by successively extending the slide approximately an inch at a time. You might have some students playing real or imaginary trumpets and others playing real or imaginary trombones. Try to get the trumpet players to depress the middle valve as the trombone players go to second (II) position; to depress the first valve as the trombone players go to third (III) position; etc. Have fun with the "musi-matics." Explain that the trumpet middle valve lowers the pitch by a half step, and the trombone second position does the same. (Use Figure 46 to go through all seven trombone positions and all the combinations of valves on the trumpet). Show, with a real trumpet if possible, how the tube coming from the middle valve (½ step valve) is short; the one coming from the first valve is a little longer (to lower the pitch a whole step); and the tube coming from the third valve is longest (to lower the pitch 1½ steps). Have your students check the mathematics of Figure 46, to see whether the combinations of valves correctly lower the pitches accordingly.

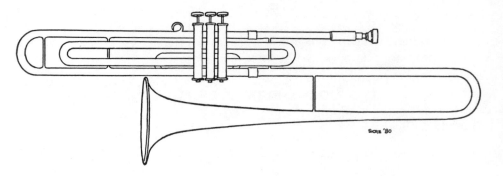

Figure 45

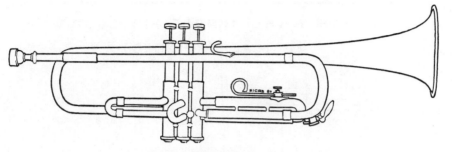

Figure 45, continued

TRUMPET AND TROMBONE FINGERINGS AND VALVE POSITIONS		
Trumpet Fingerings (o =valve depressed)	Half-steps and Steps lowered	Trombone Position Equivalent
o o o	none	I (first)
o ● o	$\frac{1}{2}$ 1 half	II (second)
● o o	1 2 halves	III (third)
● ♥ o	$1\frac{1}{2}$ 3 halves	IV (fourth)
o ● ●	2 4 halves	V (fifth)
● o ●	$2\frac{1}{2}$ 5 halves	VI (sixth)
● ● ●	3 6 halves	VII (seventh)

Figure 46

2. Have fun with "fun words," as in Figure 47, using the trumpet fingering chart. Notice that as you "write" words with the trumpet fingering patterns, you make "musical dominos" ("domi-cals?") We have had fun, with many youngsters, making even longer words such as dis-e-as-e, as in Figure 48. (We use the European system of *Dis* being D sharp, and *As* being A flat and then use the trumpet fingering to make the "musical domino.")

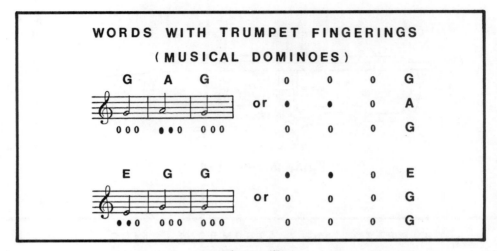

Figure 47

BUILDING WORDS WITH
TRUMPET FINGERINGS
(DIS – E – AS – E)

0	●	●	Dis (D♯)
●	●	0	E
0	●	●	As (A♭)
●	●	0	E

Figure 48

INTERVALS

Grades: 4 - 8

Concept

Many musical concepts are mathematical in nature.

Activities
&
Directions

Intervals are the same in mathematics and music—units of distance or of time. (The British use the term "interval" instead of intermission—I say!)

After placing Figure 49 on the chalkboard or on music flashcards, you might explain that an interval gets its name from the "alphabetical distance" away (e.g., from "A" to "B" is a musical 2nd; from "A" to "C" is a 3rd; "A" to "D" is a 4th). Pretty "mathe-musical," right? Oh—we forgot—you'd rather say "musi-matical!" At any rate, we have found that many students have fun using their fingers to calculate intervals. The thumb to the pointer is as "A" to "B" and therefore a 2nd. The thumb to the middle finger (A – C) is a 3rd. The thumb to the ring finger (A – D) is a 4th.

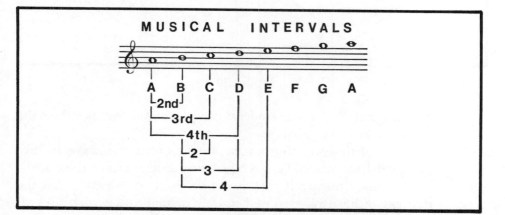

Figure 49

See if your students can figure out musical intervals.

B to C is a _____ answer: 2nd

B to D is a _____ answer: 3rd

B to E is a _____ answer: 4th

PENTATONIC AND DODECAPHONIC

Grades: 4 - 8

Concept

Music and geometry share ideas.

**Activities
  &
Directions**

1. Do your students know what the Pentagon is? A discussion of our nation's Pentagon building would be an excellent background activity for this lesson. After placing Figure 50 on the chalkboard, you might discuss our nation's military system and the Pentagon in

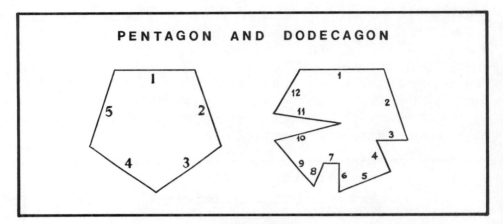

Figure 50

Washington, D.C. Some students can play naval officers, others the army, air force, or marines.

If students correctly guess, or observe, that the pentagon has five sides, can they correctly guess how many different tones there are in "pentatonic" music? If they guess correctly, or observe, that the dodecagon has twelve sides, can they name music which uses all twelve tones in Western music? (Answer: dodecaphonic music.)

2. To add humor to this activity of learning the names for five-tone or twelve-tone music, we have found that the following enjoyable activity goes over in a big way. Tell your students that, given the fact that *octave* means eight notes, the *octopus* has eight legs, and an *octagon* is an eight-sided figure, you have decided to "invent" a fictitious sea-monster with five legs called ＿＿＿＿＿＿＿? (Answer: a penta-pus) Also, since a *dodecagon* has twelve sides, and we now know that *dodecaphonic* is twelve-tone music, the sea-monster with twelve legs is ＿＿＿＿＿＿ (Answer: a dodeca-pus!)

RHYTHM RIOT — TRY IT!

Grades: 2 - 7

Materials: Apples, huckleberries, raspberries and strawberries.

Concept:

It can be fun for different rhythms to go on at the same time.

Activities
&
Directions

1. Try to give as many children as possible different rhythms, no matter how simple. Some children can even have the same rhythms, but at different *tempi* (speeds, fast or slow). Rhythms of simple songs can be used, such as "Jingle Bells" or "Hot Cross Buns." The important thing in this fun-filled rhythm riot is that the rhythms go on simultaneously!

   If your background is such that you are now drawing a blank, try saying the names of fruits to yourself (even as you read this). You will notice that you create different rhythmic patterns that have mathematical relationships. For example, AP-PLE PIE is a 2:1 or two-to-one relationship. STRAW-BER-RY PIE or RASP-BER-RY PIE is a 3:1 relationship; can you hear it? HUC-KLE-BER-RY PIE is a 4:1 relationship.

2. Figure 51 shows what these rhythms look like. Try asking your students to draw the diagram on the chalkboard. It can be fun.

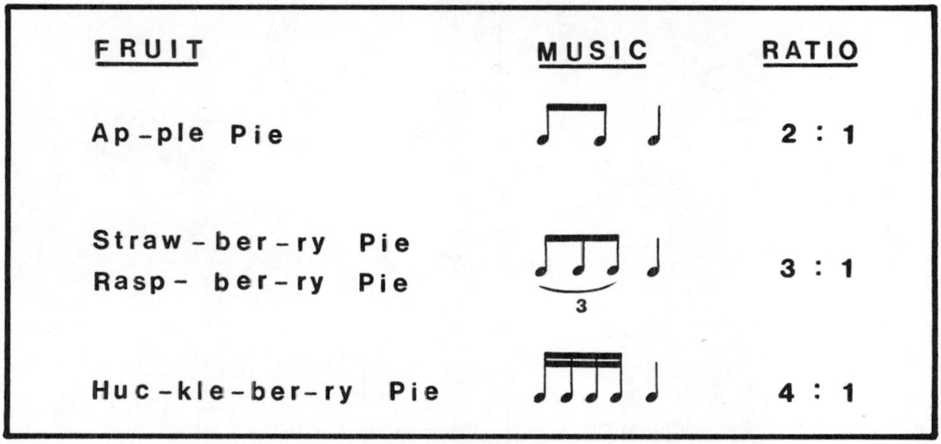

FRUIT	MUSIC	RATIO
Ap–ple Pie	♪♪ ♩	2 : 1
Straw–ber–ry Pie Rasp–ber–ry Pie	♪♪♪ ♩ (3)	3 : 1
Huc–kle–ber–ry Pie	♪♪♪♪ ♩	4 : 1

Figure 51

I'D HAVE BAKED SOME COOKIES

Grades: 3 - 6

Materials: Equipment for baking cookies; candles.

Concept

Music uses fractions.

**Activities
&
Directions**

1. Bake cookies (or have students bake cookies) with notes on them—or in the shape of notes.

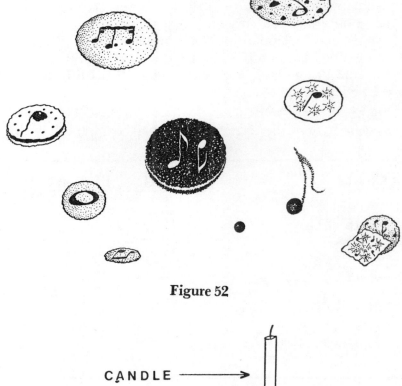

Figure 52

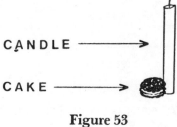

Figure 53

See if your students can identify the musical notes as eighth and sixteenth notes. An interesting discussion-debate can result from trying to figure out why an eighth note gets half of a beat.

Solution: 1/8 of what?   1/8 of *4* beats

1/8 of 4 = 4/8 = (1/2 of a beat)

2. Another activity is to bake a very small cake and make it into a quarter note by placing a small candle at the end of it. See Figure 53.

SYNCOPATION RELATION STATION

Grades: 3 - 8

Concept:

"Syncopation" means "displacement of the normal accent" or "shifting of the beat."

Activities
  &
Directions

Have a "syncopation-relation-station" where all the students try to shift the beat. Upper graders will be able to understand the concept of shifting of a beat from the normal accents (1, 2, 3, 4 for example) to the ands or in-between beats (such as 1 *and*, 2 *and*, 3 *and*, 4 *and*). Younger pupils may merely feel this type of shifting, and, of course, laugh at the rhyme of "syncopation-relation-station." For added fun, contrast some students accenting the normal beats with others accenting the in-between beats—and make this go on at the same time!

DID YOU KNOW . . .

Grades: 3 - 8

Materials: Triangle; picture of a piano keyboard.

Concept:

Music uses mathematical concepts of ratios and geometric shapes.

Activities
  &
Directions

You can explain to your pupils that the musical octave:

• is a note 8 notes higher

- sounds almost identical to a note higher or lower with the same name
- can be divided into 100 parts called *cents* (does it make sense to have *cents*—in music?!)
- arrived at through a trumpet or trombone/overtone series is "off" pitch with the same note arrived at by dividing a string in half by an interval known as the "Pythagorian Comma"

That the musical compositional technique called *counterpoint* (which produced *polyphonic* music)

- has mathematical relationships of 2:1, 3:1, and 4:1
- uses a "magic number of "9," whereby *inversions* of an *interval* is 9 minus that number

That black keys on the piano (the flats and sharps)

- are in groups of *twos* and *threes* just like a "full house"
- form a *pentatonic* or *five-note* scale

That *dodecaphonic* means

- *twelve-tone* music
- arrangements of tones in which there are 12 *equal steps* and all twelve notes have to be used

That impressionistic whole-tone music

- divides the octave into *six equal steps*
- uses mainly *four* different chords

That the triad

- is a *three*-note chord, just as the triangle is a three-sided figure and a three-sided instrument

That a *tetrachord*

- is half (or 4 notes) of the 8 note octave
- can have different relationships among its intervals

X	1 1 ½	Ionian	–	Mixolydian
Y	1 ½ 1	Dorian	–	Aeolian
Z	½ 1 1	Phrygian	–	Locrian
W	1 1 1	Lydian		

METER À LA MODE

Grades: 3 - 8

Materials: Any book that explains poetic meters and feet.

Concepts:

1. Another "mathe-musical" relationship is one of *modes* and *meters*.
2. Like the words pentagon and pentatonic, pentameter refers to five (and iambic pentameter is five groups of iambs).

Activities
&
Directions

1. Place Figure 54A on the chalkboard. Point out the iamb. Can your students tell you how many of them there are in iambic pentameter? Might they laugh when they are told that the iamb uses a silent "b" and, therefore, is pronounced "I am?" Let them laugh, of course, and let them have fun! Use this frivolity to get into a discussion of the other feet in poetry, as pictured in Figure 54A. They will probably laugh when you mention feet of poetry, for we have found that mentioning feet—even without poetry—makes children laugh.

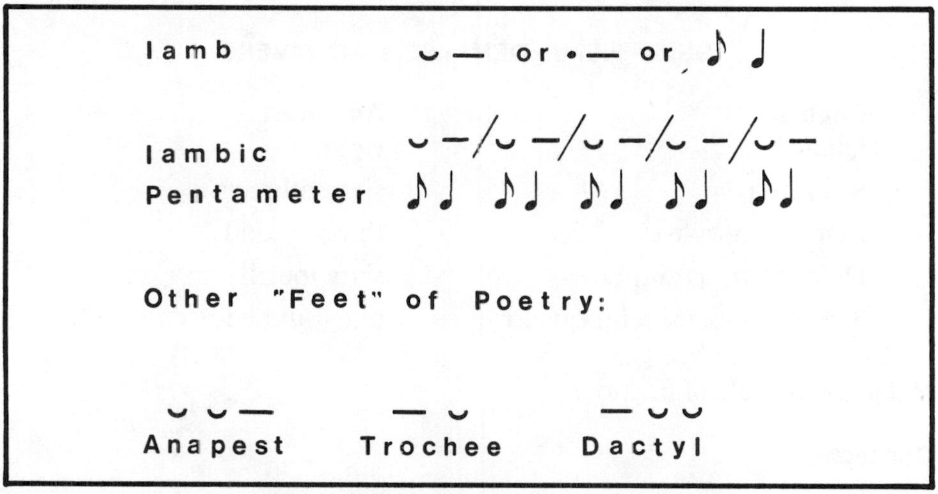

Figure 54A

2. For older students, another enjoyable activity is to go more deeply into explaining the other feet in poetry, using any helpful analogy like Morse code. You can explain that the foot consists of one stressed syllable and of either one or two unstressed syllables and the stressed syllable may either begin or end the "metrical unit." You might want to read through a great deal of poetry to see if they can discover where these relationships occur. They might discover the feet which do not come under these rules, as in Figure 54B.

---

the spondee   (- -)

the pyrrhic   (U U)

the amphibrach   (U - U)

Figure 54B

3. Using any of the metrical modes we just mentioned, have fun playing "Mèter à la Mode" in which pupils pick a mode and give it a nickname. It could be "Smokey the Trochee" or "Anapest the pest." Then, uttering silly sayings such as "I am the Iamb" they proceed to walk or clap in their metrical mode. They might rediscover how the musical, metrical modes developed.

SEMI - HEMI - DEMI - SEMI - QUAVERS

English	**American**
Quaver	eighth
Semi-quaver	sixteenth
Demi-semi-quaver	thirty-second
Hemi-demi-semi-quaver	sixty-fourth
Semi-hemi-demi-semi-quaver	one-hundred-twenty-eighth

Materials: A table of fractions.

Concepts:

1. A SHDSQ is the British way of saying a 128th note (1/128).

2. Some musical concepts are related to fractions.

Activities
&
Directions

1. Place Figure 55A on the chalkboard. Be glad when your students laugh at the funny sound of quavers, or SQ or DSQ or HDSQ or SHDSQ. We have found that a good starting point for learning about these "Mostly Music and Math" relationships is to try to "trick" your poor students into mathematical traps. One such trap is thinking of the regular multiplication table for 8, 8, 16, 24, 32, 40 instead of doubling each number after 8, 8, 16, 32, 64, 128, as a quaver is an eighth, a semi-quaver is a sixteenth, and a demi-semi-quaver is a thirty-second (each "faster" note being half of the proceeding note rather than 1/2, 1/3rd, and 1/4th, etc.).

English		American
♪	Quaver	$\frac{1}{8}$
♪ ♫	Semi-quavers	$\frac{1}{16}$
♪ ♬	Demi semi quavers	$\frac{1}{32}$
♪ ♬	Hemi-demi-semi-quavers	$\frac{1}{64}$
♪ ♬	Semi-hemi-demi-semi-quavers	$\frac{1}{128}$

Figure 55A

A semi-hemidemisemiquaver is a one-hundred-twenty-eighth note! Place Figure 55B on the chalkboard to show your pupils its other relatives.

HEMIDEMISEMIQUAVER	sixty-fourth note	♬
DEMISEMIQUAVER	thirty-second note	♬
SEMIQUAVER	sixteenth note	♪
QUAVER	eighth note	♪
CROCHET	quarter note	♩

Figure 55B

4 MINUTES 33 SECONDS
(Chance and Aleatoric Music)

Grades:

Materials: Stop watch; real or toy piano.

Concept:

Chance music is music in which you never know what is going to happen. The term *aleatoric* comes from the Latin word *alea* meaning dice.

Activities
&
Directions

1. You can play *4 Minutes 33 Seconds* by having a student go to a real or toy piano, sit down and do nothing for the specified time. The object is to listen for all the noises around you that you never really hear ordinarily: a radiator hissing, coughs, sniffles, etc. This is how the composition was first performed, as composed or designed by John Cage.

2. "Mathe-musical" fun can be had by adding up the minutes and seconds, or multiplying the number of seconds in a minute by four and adding thirty-three.

$$
\begin{array}{cc}
60 & 60 \times 4 = 240 \\
60 & + \ 33 \\
60 & \\
\underline{60} & \\
240 & \underline{} \\
\underline{33} & 273 \\
273 &
\end{array}
$$

13

More Music and ...

This chapter includes some more of the "music and's" that teachers have always enjoyed using. These "ands" are typing, crafts, science and poetry. Music and art is an old standby, of course, and music and muscles has been getting increased attention. If "making the 'funny clef' " out of wire hangers sounds appealing, this may be your favorite chapter. If baking fortune cookies that contain a musical fortune seems like fun, get ready for a fun chapter!

These and other activities, such as "find the music box" or "making a flexitone," all combine to make music fun. Why not! Remember this book's introduction? Children always have fun with music outside of school. Let us maintain a trend of making music fun in school as well!

MUSIC AND TYPING

Grades: 4 - 8

Materials: Typewriter; music paper (optional).

Concept:

Some "musical words" (words using only the musical alphabet of A B C D E F G) are also among the first letters you use when you start typing.

Activities
 &
Directions

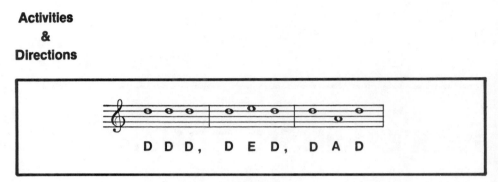

D D D, D E D, D A D

Figure 56

Place Figure 56 on the chalkboard. Use music paper, if you have it, or ask your pupils to copy Figure 60 by drawing five straight, horizontal lines on a blank sheet. You might explain that these three groups of letters are using the musical alphabet which stops at "G"—but they are also words or groups of letters that typing teachers use in their classrooms to teach one how to type. Let your students have fun practicing this. Students can take turns at the single typewriter, or, they might be inspired to bring a portable typewriter from home. Another musical game that can be combined with this activity is the game of trying to make up many small words with the musical alphabet A B C D E F G. Some of the words we have had students come up with are:

BEE	ADD	CAB
EGG	BAD	ACE
BEG	AGE	FEE
BE	BAG	FED

There are many, many more; so don't let your pupils stop after a dozen or so. After they have discovered at least forty three-letter words, let them see if they can discover which letters are closest together and, therefore, best for teaching touch typing. Have fun comparing the words they have discovered with those in a standard beginning typing book.

MAKING THE FUNNY CLEF

Grades: 1 - 8

Materials: Wire and/or wooden hangers; clay or other modeling compound.

Activities
 &
Directions

Break the top off a wire or wooden hanger. Very often, the top wire part comes right off a wooden hanger and looks like Figure 57.

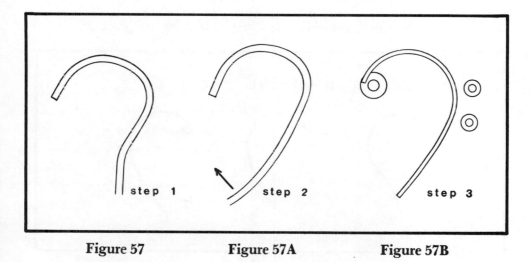

Figure 57   **Figure 57A**   **Figure 57B**

Then, just bend it so that it looks like Figure 57A

Now, add some clay to the tip so that it looks like Figure 57B. We call Figure 57B the "funny clef," to reinforce that it is the "F" clef, and to differentiate it from the G clef as in Figure 58.

Figure 58

The whole procedure can now be visualized by looking at Figure 59.

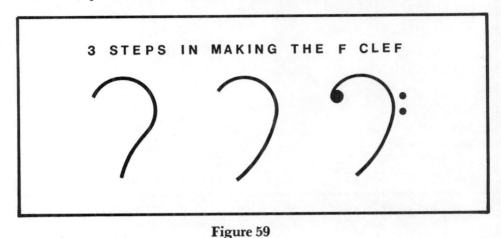

Figure 59

LET'S PLAY WITH CLAY TODAY

Grades: 3 - 8

Activity: Take a bobby pin from a student; and break it in two. Now bend it so that it looks like Figure 60, minus the "head." Take a small ball of clay and place at the bottom of the bent bobby pin so that it now looks like the eighth note in Figure 60.

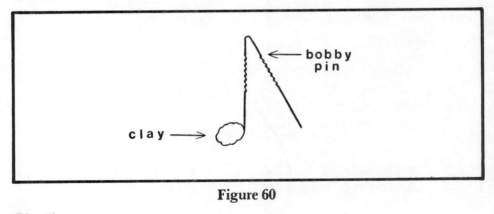

Figure 60

**Directions
&
Questions:**

Does anyone have a bobby pin?

Can anyone bend and break this so that it looks like the diagram on the chalkboard? (Figure 60 minus the "head.")

Here is a small piece of clay. Watch where I place it.

Does this look like the picture on the board? What type of a note is this? That's right, an eighth note.

MUSIC AND SCIENCE

Grades: 3 - 8

Materials: Pictures of caves and stalagmites: a guitar; thin and thick rubber bands; a toy or real trombone; pictures of a tuba; large and small drums.

Concept

Music reflects many of nature's laws of science.

HAVE YOU HEARD:

1. The story of finding in a Bavarian cave, eight stalagmites which when struck with a stone gave out a perfect diatonic octave?

   • Explain what a stalagmite is—using the idea of "g" for ground and "c" for ceiling (in stala*c*tite).

   • Review the octave as having eight notes such as A - A (ABC-DEFGA) or B - B (BCDEFGAB). You might explain it as a distance or interval that can be broken into eight parts, or as the duplication of a tone higher or lower but sounding almost identical (students call it . . . the same note only higher").

2. The instrument called "the flexitone"?

   • You and your students might make this simple instrument which clearly demonstrates that when a vibrating object vibrates faster, the faster vibrations-per-second (v.p.s.) produce a higher pitch.

   • The flexitone has been defined as a piece of flexible steel fastened to a handle and set in vibration by hammers attached to both sides. The player shakes the flexitone to produce a musical sound, raising the pitch by pressing on the steel with his thumb, and lowering it by relieving the pressure. Small flexitones are used chiefly as rattles, but the larger ones produce a really lovely, ethereal tone, and used to be common in dance bands.

DID YOU KNOW:

1. That thicker strings produce lower or deeper tones? The principle is that thicker strings vibrate more slowly; the slower or fewer vibrations, the deeper the pitch.
   - Demonstrate that a thick rubber band will produce a deeper sound than one which is thin, provided the thick rubber band is not stretched too tightly.
   - Explain that v. p. s. means vibrations-per-second, and that: more vibrations-per-second produce a high sound or pitch and fewer vibrations-per-second produce a deep or low sound or pitch.

   You might show your students how thick the lower strings of the guitar are, or the lowest string of the double bass.

2. That long instruments also produce low, deep sounds?
   - Get a long, long toy trombone that has a deep sound.
   - Show pictures of the large tuba and the contrabassoon.
   - Encourage students to bring in any kind of drum they might have at home. Borrow drums of different sizes from the music department or another school. Line up the drums according to size beginning with the smallest ones. Let students have fun discovering that the larger drums have the deepest tones.

3. That with the pre-electric phonograph
   - you started with a sound, say of a violin, and the vibrations of air that constituted this sound were said to be "evanescent"?
   - this evanescent sound was converted into motions of a stylus;
   - this motion—still said to be transitory—was recorded in a disc of wax, a permanent physical form;
   - the listener then used a device which translated the physical characteristics of the wax disc into motions of another stylus;
   - the motions of this stylus were in turn converted back into atmospheric vibrations which gave approximately the sensation of the original sound.

We have always found that pupils are amazed by this story. Moreover, if you can obtain some very old 78 records, they will have even more fun as they hear the funny sounds. The most fun of all, of course, is when someone can obtain an old windup RCA Victrola on which to play the very old recordings.

FIND THE BELLS

Grades: 3 - 8

Materials: Bells of all types (wind, dinner, cat, cow, church).

Concepts:

1. There are many different types of bells.
2. Bells evolved from plates or pots that were banged.

Activities
&
Directions

Try to motivate your students to have fun rummaging through flea markets and garage sales for all kinds of music boxes and bells. Of course, we know that being "bitten" by the flea market bug (pun intended) is something that occurs later on in life. However, we have found that pupils often come back with many different bells (from many different places) and tell us that they had lots of fun searching for them—and then ringing them! Years later, some students come back to say hello and tell us that we started them on their bell collections!

FIND THE MUSIC BOX

Grades: K - 8

Materials: Books on music boxes such as Alec Templeton's *Music Boxes* (New York: Wilfred Funk), 1958; David Tallis's *Music Boxes, A Guide for Collectors* (New York: Stein and Day); and R. DeWaard, *From Music Boxes to Street Organs*, translated from Dutch by Wade Jenkins (the Vestal Press), 1967.

Concepts:

1. Music boxes were used to mechanically create music, before recordings.
2. Music boxes play different types of music such as marches, waltzes, or lullabies.

Activities
    &
Directions

1. Before recordings, piano rolls and organ books were used to play entire overtures and symphonies. There are books available which show how these books and rolls were "punched out" so that the piano or organ could play mechanically. You might discuss this as background, to set the stage for some discussion of how music boxes work. To inject some humor, you might want to add that at one time a small type of barrel organ was used to teach canaries to sing! There were also mechanical banjos and zithers, and mechanical accordions. There were even mechanical singing birds in cages, and—of course—the popular mechanical organ grinders and monkeys that were patterned after the real organ grinders who would walk about with pet monkeys on their shoulders.

2. To play the game of "Find the Music Box," younger students can first ask their parents to buy them toys that can be wound up to play tunes. Perhaps they have some already. Older students can do more searching themselves. Perhaps their parents have old toys or devices in the attic. Perhaps their relatives or friends have some. Some books show excellent colored pictures of jeweled music boxes or ornate music boxes to hold jewelry in them. Is it possible that any of your children's parents have one of these? Anyway, games can be played with music boxes or musical toys that are similar to hiding the board eraser.

POETRY AND MUSIC

Grades: K - 6

Materials: Poetry in different languages about music (a librarian's help will be needed); toy instruments; pictures of marching bands; pictures of owls and roosters.

Concept:

Musical ideas can be approached through poetry.

Activities
    &
Directions

Using poetry to introduce musical ideas can be fun. Teachers and students who might ordinarily shy away from words such as musical imitation or musical counterpoint will be much more easily persuaded to approach the subject through poetry. Students who will readily read Sitwell's *On Hearing Four Bands Play at Once in a Public Square*, may not be so easily persuaded to sing "Three Blind Mice," "Row, Row, Row Your Boat," or "Frère Jacques."

Describing musical noises through imitative poetry can also be enjoyable. Reading poems that imitate musical sounds can precede actual experimentation with real musical noises. Children love the poetic "baroom" or "kling klang."

This area has been thoroughly researched and many pupils have told us that the process can be a great deal of fun. Many teachers have attested to the fact that musicality is enhanced rather than detracted from. Reticent students are brought into the fold of creativity, so to speak. Students who are not yet musically inventive begin to lose some of their inhibitions.

> *If a pun*
> *is fun,*
> *we've won!*

There are many types of poetry that teachers use to conjure up images of music. Much of it is pure fun! And one type, imitative, doesn't even have to be in English. Imitative words, often invented for the purpose, are useful, especially for suggestion of the noise instruments. A good example is Detlev von Liliencron's *Die Musik Kommt* (Samtliche Werke von Detlev von Liliencron (Berlin, n.d.), VII, 51-52). The poem describes a military band moving through a little German village; first the approaching sound, then the children peering out at them from doors and windows, and finally the sound dying away in the distance. Even if you don't read German, see if you can't conjure up this image when reading part of this poem.

> *Klingling, tchingtching und Paukenkrach,*
> *Noch aus der Ferne tönt es schwach,*
> *Ganz leise bumbumbumbum tching,*
> *Zog da ein bunter Schmetterling,*
> * Tchingtching, bum, um die Ecke?*

Do you think your students will be able to "get through" this part of the poem? With a little coaching from you, they will. If not, here it is in English.

> *Klingling, chingching and kettledrums,*
> *Still from the distance softly comes,*
> *Quite faintly, boom-boom-boom-boom ching—*
> *Did a gay butterfly take wing,*
> * Chingching, boom, round the corner?*

You might stage the parade, dividing the class into "readers" and "marchers." Real or imaginary instruments can be used, and the imaginary kind provide an opportunity for pantomime. Have you ever seen the play with music, *Every Good Boy Deserves Favour*, in which one of the two jailed men (supposedly insane) hears an imaginary orchestra in his head?

Other poems conjure up images of music.

If we admit the crowing cock as a musical sound (it was used in Bach's *St. Matthew Passion*), Coleridge's *Christabel* gives us a nice image along with material for pantomime. See if your students don't have fun with this one.

> *'This the middle of the night by the*
> *castle clock,*
> *And the owls have awakened the*
> *crowing cock,*
> *Tu- - whit! - - Tu-.-whoo!*
> *And hark again! the crowing cock,*
> *How drowsily it crew.*

HAPPY FACES

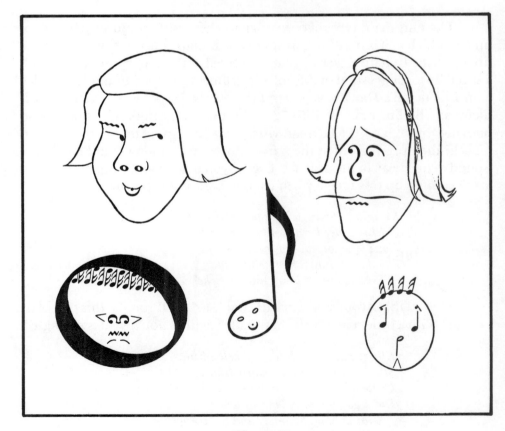

Figure 61

Grades: K - 6

Concepts:

1. The tie.
2. Counting rhythms.

Activities
   &
Directions

Place Figure 61 on the chalkboard. Younger children should have fun looking at notes used as eyes and mouths, or seeing a music note with a face on it. Older children might snicker, but, in our experience, will have fun drawing Figure 61. Another activity is to add up the total number of beats in "Happy Faces," using the chart provided in Figure 62.

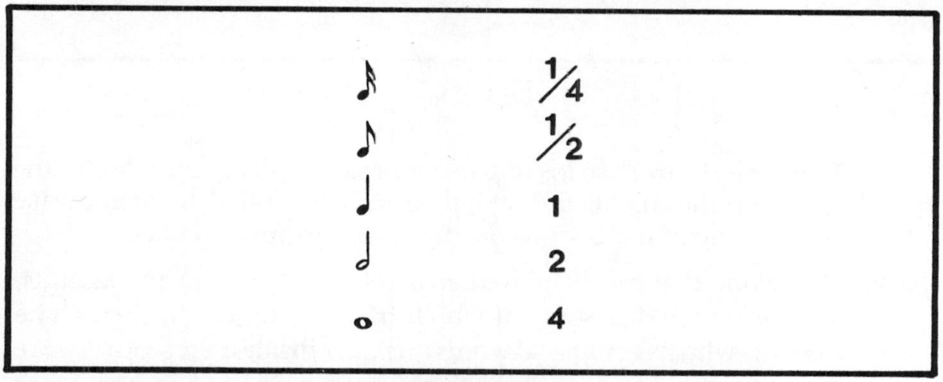

♪	$\frac{1}{4}$
♪	$\frac{1}{2}$
♩	1
♩	2
o	4

Figure 62

FORTUNE COOKIES

Grades: K - 4

Materials: Torn pieces of paper or strips of paper ½″ by 3″.

Concepts:

1. Children's antics can be made into educational games.
2. Fortune cookies can have musical messages instead of philosophical ones.

Activities
   &
Directions

Place Figure 63 on the chalkboard.

```
              F O R T U N E      C O O K I E S

         F    clef            C  –  larinet

         O  –  pera           O  –  boe

         R  –  hythm          O  –  ctave

         T  –  rumpet         K  –  lavier

         U  –  nison          I  –  ntermezzo

         N  –  otes           E  –  tude

         E  –  legy           S  –  piccato
```

Figure 63

Distribute ½″ by 3″ strips of paper and ask pupils to copy one of the words on the chalkboard with their initials. Collect them and bake some of them into biscuits or (if you can) fortune cookies.

2. One game that can be played is as follows: Give out the biscuits, muffins or cookies, some of which have "fortunes" in them. The students who have musical words on paper inside their food treat are semi-finalists. They now have to play an elimination contest. Since all children love to crumple and throw little pieces of paper, why not capitalize on this universal "problem" and turn the "problem" into a plus? Structure and supervise their crumpling and throwing musical fortunes at someone else. The one catching the "music balls" is "out" if the paper is dropped. If the word is a musical word, the successful catcher gets a prize.

MUSIC AND MUSCLES

Grades: 2 - 6

Materials: Books on carillon playing; pictures of a carillon.

Concept

A *carillonneur* is one who rings the sets of church bells known as the carillon.

Activities
&
Directions

Explain that *carillonics* may be more like an athletic event than some-one making sweet music, and describe a *carilloneur* at work. Many teachers have found that it makes their students laugh and do pantomime. Watch their reactions as you explain that often the *carilloneur* was bathed in sweat and every muscle of his body seemed at full tension! (He had to grapple the huge pedal bells with his feet, and with gloved hands had to rapidly manipulate two rows of keyed pegs! After a brief breathing pause, he might astonish you with *bravura* (virtuoso) playing, working the huge nine-ton and six-ton bells for the melody with his feet, while playing very, very fast sixteenth and even thirty-second notes on the treble bells!) Does it sound to your students that a job like that is fun? It certainly is strenuous, isn't it? Why not have a lively discussion of just how difficult it is. You know the way children have fun arguing: "I bet it is harder than . . ."

WHAT WOULD THE WORLD BE LIKE WITHOUT MUSIC?

Grades: 2 - 8

Materials: Jump rope; drum sticks.

Concept:

Music plays a vital role in almost every aspect of our lives.

Activities
&
Directions

1. Ask your pupils to describe what they think the world would be like without:
   - radios
   - dancing
   - discos
   - bands
   - Muzak
   - background music for television
   - music in a movie
   - football half-times
   - the racetrack bugle call

2. Many teachers have found that their students enjoy playing a game of "What If?"

Directions: pantomime the following activities,

- turn off the sound to television—act bored!
- turn on the radio, but no sound comes on and you are bored!
- dance without music, and then act disgusted!
- make believe you were playing the drums but no sound came out!
- skip rope but without the singing or clapping
- the sound of music suddenly comes back and *everything is fun again!*

WHAT WILL YOU DO THIS SUMMER?

Grades: K - 8

Materials: Brochures on music festivals; programs from camp plays; recorders and harmonicas; travel posters.

Concept:

Summer is a wonderful time for musical fun.

Activities
  &
Directions

Is it possible that summer is finally around the corner? Are your students beginning to talk about what they will do on vacation? And, important, are you starting to share their enthusiasm? Why not! In some ways, June is almost a culmination of two or three months of very mixed feelings about whether you want to be indoors or out. Well—quite soon that decision will be taken out of our hands and we all will be enjoying the fields, or the beach, or the lake, or the woods, or whatever it is that we do when we're not in school. Your job, musically, is to suggest ways in which the summer experience can be enriched musically.

FESTIVALS

Ask your pupils to begin thinking about summer fairs and festivals. There are jazz festivals, ethnic celebrations, and bluegrass music festivals. Many of them start in June, but then again many school districts let out early. You might suggest that your pupils ask their parents to check newspapers and bulletin board listings for which festivals are in your area. For example, are you near any of the following or are there any like these near you?

Fiesta de san Antonio: ceremonial dances and Ghost dances done by Tigua Indians.

Bavarian Festivals: such as the ones in Frankenmuth, Minnesota, or Haines Falls, New York. There is good food as well as traditional music (as it has been preserved in this country with Polka bands, etc.).

Jazz Festivals: such as the Hampton Jazz Festival in Hampton, Virginia, or the gigantic Newport Jazz Festival (that moved to New York and Saratoga after it left Rhode Island).

International Country Music Fan Fair: such as the one in Nashville.

National Oldtime Fiddlers Contest and Festival: such as the one in Weiser (Idaho).

Beanblossom Bluegrass Music Festival: such as the one in Martinsville (Indiana).

Ethnic Celebrations: such as the Tabor, South Dakota, celebration to honor its Czechoslavakian heritage, including singing, dancing and polka music; the Danish and Swedish festivals in Minden and Stromsburg, Nebraska, including traditional polkas and mazurkas.

These are but a few, and you and your pupils can probably list many more.

CAMP

Get your pupils to smile by thinking of all the fun they can have with music in camp: singing around the campfire; playing guitar, flute, recorder, harmonica or other easy-to-carry instruments that are frequently seen at outdoor gatherings. Some students will want to just sit on the grass and listen to music that is being played in the background. And what about dancing? Ask them to list their favorite current dances or their favorite recordings. Older pupils may want to think of their girlfriends and boyfriends at a camp party, dancing with each other.

Camp plays are also fun, and your pupils may want to think of which ones they might like to put on at camp.

TRAVEL

Many pupils do some traveling during the summer. Often it is not very extensive; but some students take long trips to far away and interesting places. Students who know where they will be going might want to give reports on their itinerary (and you might be able to bring in music for the countries to which they will be going). This is usually both fun and challenging. Travel posters can be placed around the room for added stimulation.

14

A Baker's Dozen of Fun Activities

**SMILE SONGS
AND
ORIGINAL PARODIES**

TO THE TUNE OF "Down in the Valley"

*When you are happy, smile ear to ear
Smile if you're thinking, "what should I wear?"*

*When you are happy, smile ear to ear
If you are eating or combing your hair*

*When you are happy, smile ear to ear
Even if you meet an old grizzly bear*

*When you are happy, smile ear to ear
Pretend you're wealthy and haven't a care*

*When you are happy, smile ear to ear
Even if glue has been put in your hair*

*When you are happy, smile ear to ear
Even if they've put a tack on your chair!*

*When you are happy, smile ear to ear
And never answer "I bet" or "I dare!"*

TO THE TUNE OF "My Hat It Has Three Corners"

My trumpet it has three valves
Yes three valves my trumpet has
And if you like the trumpet
Then you probably like jazz

Yes my trumpet it has three valves
If it didn't it might be
A bugle in a drum corps
Rather than in a symphony

The trumpet valves are funny
When you press them they come up
And trumpets can be muted
In the bell you place a cup

The first valve is a B flat
Or an F and sometimes D
And if you play two valves down
You get C-sharp, A, or E

The second and the third valves
Help you play E or A flat
And we find this as much fun
As swinging a baseball bat.

(Can you write more?)

TO THE TUNE OF "There's a Hole at the Bottom of the Sea"

There's a violin on the bottom of the sea,
There's a violin on the bottom of the sea,
There's a vi - o -lin
There's a violin on the bottom of the sea

There's a case for the violin . . . etc.

There's a neck on the violin in the case . . . etc.

There's a peg on the neck of the violin in the case
. . . etc.

There's a string on the peg on the neck of the violin
in the case . . . etc.

There's a bow on the string on the peg on the neck
of the violin in the case . . . etc.

There's rosin on the bow on the string on the peg on
the neck of the violin in the case . . . etc.

Paid a dollar for the rosin on the bow . . . etc.

Where's my money for the rosin on the bow . . . etc.

TO THE TUNE OF "Roll Out the Barrel"

PULL OUT MY BARREL my clarinet barrel's
  stuck
PULL OUT MY BARREL my clarinet barrel's
  stuck
PULL OUT MY BARREL my clarinet barrel's
  stuck

Next time use some cork grease on it
And it won't get stuck

My valve is sluggish, it won't come up all the way
My valve is sluggish, it won't come up all the way
My valve is sluggish, it won't come up all the way

Next time use a little valve oil
And it will come up

CAN YOU COMPLETE?

TO THE TUNE OF "The Twelve Days of Christmas"

On the first day of Christmas my true love gave to me
A washboard and a monochord

On the second day of Christmas my true love gave to
  me
Two flute duets and a washboard and a monochord

On the third day . . .
Three new kazoos, two flute duets and a washboard
  and a monochord

On the fourth day . . .
Four French horns _____

On the fifth day . . .
Five staff lines _____

On the sixth day . . .
Six guitar strings _____

(to be completed)

TO THE TUNE OF "This Old Man"

*This old man he played one, he played solo
  flutophone
With a He-mi, Demi, Semi-Quaver note
Look at all the songs I wrote.*

*This old man he played two, he played two on
  his kazoo
With a He-mi, De-mi, Semi-Quaver note
Look at all the songs I wrote.*

(to be completed)

HAVE YOU EVER?

- sung "Row, Row, Row Your Boat" and really made believe you were rowing?
- sung "Are You Sleeping" or "Frére Jacques" and acted it out while singing it?
- acted out "Three Blind Mice"?

PANTOMIME ACTIVITIES

For "Row, Row, Row Your Boat," five students sit on chairs and make believe they are in a boat rowing. Several other students, or the rest of the class, make the sounds of water.

For "Are You Sleeping" or "Frère Jacques," one student lies on the floor, making believe he or she is asleep; another makes believe he is Brother John's superior who is asking the question "Are you sleeping?" and other students make believe they are ringing the bells.

For "Three Blind Mice," some of the students are the three mice, one girl is the farmer's daughter. Make sure you use something very dull to represent the carving knife with which she cuts off their tails.

CAN YOU SING . . .

Like:

- a frog?
- a bird?
- an organ grinder?
- a barber?

- a cheerleader?
- a marching marine?
- a lumberjack?
- a cave man?

As if:

- you have marbles in your mouth?
- you are dying?
- you are on a pirate ship?
- you are hoisting the sails?
- you are in the bathtub or shower?
- you are a recording star?
- you are in the church choir?
- you are on a boat ride?
- you're around a camp fire, on a picnic?

Some of these images will make your students laugh (which is what you want, of course, so they can loosen up); all of them will conjure up a different image.

UNDERLINE THE WORD

Directions: Underline the words you see in these musical words or composer's names.

		Answer
1.	Handel	Handel
2.	Palestrina	Palestrina
3.	Beethoven	Beethoven
4.	Wagner	Wagner
5.	Tchaikovsky	Tchaikovsky
6.	Schumann	Schumann
7.	Mussorgsky	Mussorgsky
8.	Haydn	Haydn
9.	accordion	accordion
10.	baton	baton
11.	Copland	Copland

NUMBERS IN MUSIC

2 — Duet, Duo

3 — Trio, Triad, Triangle, Movements in a Concerto

4 — Quartet, Tetrachord, Movements in a Symphony, strings on violin, spaces on the staff

5 — Pentatonic scale, Black keys on the piano, lines on the staff

6 — Notes in the whole-tone scale, strings on the guitar

WHAT PART OF AN INSTRUMENT WOULD YOU USE:

	Answer	Instrument
1. To open a door?	Keys	Piano, Saxophone, Flute, Clarinet
2. To cross a river?	Bridge	Cello, Violin, Viola
3. To tie a package?	String	Guitar, Double Bass
4. In a playground?	Slide	Trombone
5. To keep your shirt closed?	Buttons	Accordion
6. For pickles?	Barrel	Clarinet
7. To steal?	Crook	Bassoon
8. With an arrow?	Bow	Violin, Viola
9. With a formal tuxedo?	Hi-hat (cymbal)	Drum set
10. To help you find your livestock?	Cowbell	Percussion

MORE RIDDLES, TEASERS, AND ONE-LINERS

Q.   What composer's name rhymes with house or mouse?
A.   Strauss (Richard or Johann).

Q.   What musical instrument uses a thief?
A.   The bassoon; it uses a *crook*.

Q.   What instrument rhymes with bellow?
A.   The *cello*.

Q.   Which cartoon character can best "carry a tune"?
A.   Superman.

Q.   Which composer can honestly say: "to be perfectly Frank"?
A   César Franck, a French composer.

Q.   What type of an oven is musical?
A.   A Beeth-*oven*.

Q.   Which art is most musical?
A.   Moz-*art*.

Q.   Name a musical shoe
A.   *Schu*-mann

Q.   What famous composer's name translates into Joe Green?
A.   Giuseppi Verdi

Q.   What composer has another famous composer's name (Verdi) in it?
A.   Monte-verdi.

or

Q.   Take a famous composer of opera, add a prefix, and which other composer do you get?
A.   Monte-verdi.

HELPING YOUR STUDENTS TO LEARN INSTRUMENT SIZE

Q.   Which instrument might Tom Thumb play?
A.   The piccolo.

Q.   Which instrument might Paul Bunyan or the Jolly Green Giant play?
A.   The tuba, contrabass clarinet, or double bass.

THE 1812 OVERTURE

1. Take the number of notes in a pentatonic scale (Hint: same number as the sides in a pentagon.)   5

2. Add the number of players in a quartet. $+4$
        ___
        9

3. Double it. $\times 2$
        ___

4. Next to this number, write the number of notes in a chromatic scale or dodecaphonic music (Hint: same number as inches to the foot.)   18

        12

5. The answer should be a famous overture by Tchaikovsky that has the same date as a famous American War with England.   18 and 12

        1812

CITY FUN SONGS

Having fun with music in the city is best described in *City Scene* by Alfred Balkin. The musical score and cassette recording are published by Now View Music, 17 West 60th Street—8th Floor, New York, New York 10023. Some fun songs in this collection:

Walk the Block

Feeding Pigeons

Siren Song

Sounds (of the City)

Traffic Jam

One Push of the Button

What's the Solution (to Pollution)?

Another song experience for children is *We Live In The City* by Alfred Balkin. Materials include stereo LP record, piano accompaniment, Teacher's Guide and song sheet. Some of the selections are as follows:

Many Streets

People Rushing

A Big Apartment House

Skyscrapers

I Like to Ride the Elevator

The above work can be obtained by writing

> Theodore Presser Co.
> Bryn Mawr, Pa, 19010

Reaching and Teaching Through Music (Series) by Alfred Balkin is an original art and music audio-visual series. There are six songs in each package. Each package consists of six film strips, six cassettes and a Teacher's Guide which includes melodies, chord symbols and lyrics plus interdisciplinary teaching suggestions for each song. The series can be purchased from

> Oak Woods Media
> 2043 S. 11th Street
> Kalamazoo, Mi. 49009

The piano score is available from

> Now View Music
> 170 N. E. 33rd Street
> Ft. Lauderdale, Fl. 33334

NEW MUSIC GAMES

A new musical set of games that·students can play is called *MUSIC!!* There are three sets of games. Each set deals with rhythmic pattern recognition.

- Each game is played like bingo.
- Each game has cards, markers and a cassette tape.

The games, *MUSIC!!*, can be ordered from Oregon Music Materials, 2535 Charnelton Street, Eugene, Oregon 97405.

Another game, *Connquiz*, teaches listening skills. This game is also played like bingo. The listener is asked to identify dances, instruments, and other aspects of music. We have found it to be very effective and fun for the students.

Connquiz is published by C. G. Conn, Ltd. of Elkhart, Indiana 46516, and is available through them.

TIC TAC "DO"

This is played like Tic Tac Toe, but with a sharp as the gameboard and flats and naturals instead of circles and crosses.

Index